Poetry as Prayer:
The Hound of Heaven

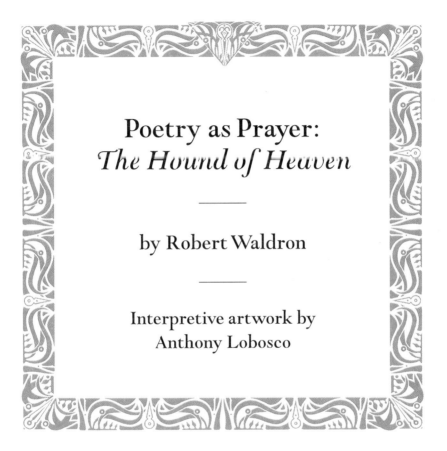

Poetry as Prayer:
The Hound of Heaven

———

by Robert Waldron

———

Interpretive artwork by
Anthony Lobosco

Pauline
BOOKS & MEDIA
BOSTON

Library of Congress Cataloging-in-Publication Data

Waldron, Robert G.
    Poetry as Prayer : The hound of heaven / by Robert
Waldron ; foreword by M. Basil Pennington ; interpretive
artwork by Anthony Lobosco.
      p.   cm.
    Includes bibliographical references.
    ISBN 0-8198-5914-1 (pbk.)
    1. Thompson, Francis, 1859–1907.   Hound of heaven.
2. Religious poetry,   English—History and criticism.
3. Prayer.   I. Thompson, Francis, 1859–1907.   Hound of
heaven.   II. Title.
PR5650.H63W35   1999
821´.8—dc21   99–12708
                                             CIP

Printed and published in the U.S.A. by Pauline Books & Media,
50 Saint Paul's Avenue, Boston, MA 02130-3491.

www.pauline.org

Pauline Books & Media is the publishing house of the Daughters of
St. Paul, an international congregation of women religious serving
the Church with the communications media.

2 3 4 5 6   04 03 02 01 00

Dedicated to
Margaret C. Waldron

Contents

Foreword

Francis Thompson has always been one of the significant poets in my life. I think each one of us who have let his *Hound of Heaven* speak to us cannot but feel that two lives have intersected at a very deep level—that Thompson has caught hold of and expressed with magnificent beauty and profound insight some of the deepest reality of our own lives. Thompson, who spoke of himself as the Poet of the Return to God, saw the universal experience of erring humanity incarnated in his own personal experience and gave intensely poignant expression to this. Robert Waldron invites us to enter more deeply into this experience and in an artful commentary opens it out for us.

But Waldron has given us something much more than a rich, inviting and insightful commentary on one of the greatest Christian poems ever written. In his first chapter Waldron opens up for us a whole dimension of the role of poetry in our lives that most of us never heard about in our college courses. He invites us to enter into the silence and solitude of the hermitage of poetry where the total attention it calls forth enables us to escape from our usual self-centeredness. We come to a moment of self-lessness that is the space for epiphany—to use James Joyce's expression—an epiphany that can illumine our darkness, touch on the Divine and give us a whole new understanding of ourselves. Call it prayer if you will but it is certainly as far from saying "prayers" as are the choirs of the heavens from our Sunday hymns. It is a dimension of poetry especially meaningful in these millennium days of spiritual renewal when the quest for a sure path inward and beyond is being eagerly sought by so many.

Perhaps many of us rarely give ourselves over to poetry. Not so much because it is "soul work" as because such an encounter with Reality inevitably demands of us conversion. Through the poetic experience we come to experience the deeper, fuller, richer possibility of life and are confronted with the folly of our superficiality and self-centeredness. We are insistently and powerfully beckoned by true poetry to live more fully in the light and vibrancy of Reality. This demands a dying to the false self we have constructed, that false self made up of what I do, what I have, what others think of me, and a courageous entering into the wondrous realms of the true self, the self that is the image of God, of Divine Beauty, ever coming forth from God's inexhaustible creative love. Frightening! Exciting! Daring to live such an adventure needs a companion. And this is what the poet can offer us.

Our Lord said: You judge a tree by its fruit. Waldron has marshaled a most impressive array of great souls who have found their way into the celebration of their own greatness through poetry. Some he only names; with others he shares a bit of their fascinating journey.

My hope is that this book will not only reach the "converted"—those already attuned to the sacredness of poetry and its potential—but will also reach the "searchers"—those who have yet to find the One they are seeking. May all of us experience a true epiphany in the Lord.

M. Basil Pennington, OCSO
St. Joseph's Abbey
Spencer, MA

Acknowledgments

I wish to thank the following, without whom this book would never have come to light:

Brother Edward O'Donnell, OCD
Reverend Patrick Brown, OSCO
Madonna Therese Ratliff, FSP
Mary Mark Wickenhiser, FSP
Helen Rita Lane, FSP
and

Dr. Paul Mariani,
Distinguished Professor of Literature at
the University of Massachusetts

Introduction

Poetry as literature.

Poetry as art.

Poetry as inspiration.

Poetry as enlightenment.

Why not poetry as prayer?

The thought occurred to me one night as I drove home from my job teaching high school literature. The poetry we had been studying mirrored so much of life: days of love and contentment, days of pain and loneliness; the pinnacles of bliss and the darkness of heartbreak. Whatever we've experienced in life, we can be sure that somewhere out there, a poet has known the same and has captured those feelings in words both eloquent and poignant.

So why not use those words to reflect on our lives, and allow poetry to draw us closer to God in prayer?

Poetry used as prayer offers the unique opportunity for the "pray-er" to be touched at the deepest spiritual level, and to be changed by another person's transforming experience. Indeed, as prayer, poetry's power to transform is particularly noteworthy, because it can lead to an epiphanic encounter with the Divine.

Epiphany: A Spiritual Turning Point

A notion of epiphany can be abstracted from the fiction of James Joyce. In Joyce's *Stephen Hero,* Stephen describes epiphany as "a sudden spiritual manifestation, whether in the vulgarity of speech or of gesture or in a memorable phase of the mind itself. It is for the man of letters to record these epiphanies with extreme care, seeing that they themselves are the most delicate and evanescent moments."

Here, epiphany means the insight of self-knowledge. Joyce uses the event of the Epiphany, when the three kings visited the Christ Child, to express a unique moment of awareness. For Joyce, this moment is similar to gazing upon the Divine, which for the Magi, was a life-enhancing moment, one that possessed the power of transformation.

Lately I have come to realize, however, that epiphany is more than a literary term and more profound than the mere acquisition of insight. Epiphany is an exquisite moment of radiance whose numinous quality possesses the power to wrench one out of one's self. It is a brief illumination, an insight whose transformative power is instantaneous, whose aftereffects forever linger in the soul. In such a moment there is simultaneously a self-forgetting and an uplifting· intellectually, spiritually and sometimes physically, one wants to shout and dance for joy!

Poetry, when used as prayer, offers a unique opportunity for the "pray-er" to experience an epiphany in one or more of its vital features:

Beauty: Epiphany's beauty draws us out of ourselves.

Suddenness: Epiphany is entirely unexpected.

Attention: Epiphany pierces our soul with rapt attention.

Insight: Epiphany gives insight into deeper meanings.

Joy: Epiphany moves us to joy and to serenity.

Sacred: Epiphany is a gift from God, a moment of grace.

Any of us may be moved by the music of Mozart or a painting by Vermeer or a poem by Francis Thompson. It is an aesthetic experience bringing pleasure and beauty into our lives. Epiphany, according to this definition, is simultaneously an aesthetic and spiritual manifestation:

God's presence renders what would ordinarily be a merely aesthetic event into one that is sacred. Thus, in my prayer life, poetry assumes a tremendous importance because my epiphanies have most often been related to verse in which I have been immersed.

Thomas Merton once wrote regarding the spiritual potential of all art:

> Art enables us to find ourselves and lose ourselves at the same time. The mind that responds to the intellectual or spiritual values that lie hidden in a poem, a painting or a piece of music, discovers a spiritual vitality. This vitality lifts the mind above itself, takes it out of itself, and makes it present on a level of being that it did not know it could ever achieve.[1]

I hope the following pages devoted to the life of Francis Thompson and his most famous and moving poem, *The Hound of Heaven*, will prove in some way to be an epiphanic experience for all who read this book and who desire to begin a journey with poetry as prayer.

Chapter 1

Why Poetry?

Why read poetry? Not long ago this question was hurled at me by one of my high school students who lamented that poetry required more effort and attention to understand than her usual reading assignments of short stories, essays and novels. I empathized with her frustration and began to ponder her question. Of course, the unspoken question was, "What's in it for me?" Little did she realize that her question was aimed at my very vocation as a teacher and my very being as a person; not only is poetry an important part of my curriculum, it is also an integral part of my inner life.

Poetry's Beauty

Since then I've given much thought to her question. Today I would say to this student that we read poetry because it is beautiful, and beauty is as essential to our spirit as breath is to our body. We read poetry because, as poet and critic Samuel Taylor Coleridge observes, it is "the best words in the best order." "Best words" suggest the union of sound and sense, a marriage whose "best order" brings poetry to life. I'd also say that we too are co-creators every time we read poetry. Poem and reader become one in an act of attention. When the reader and the poem meet for the first time there are infinite possibilities for enrichment, if not epiphany. We also read poetry because it is pleasurable, a pleasure derived from rhythm, repetition and rhyme, and from imagery, thought and emotion.

We also read poetry because it awakens us to the beauty of the natural world around us, God's gift to us. Poets worth their salt shout "Look!" Poets, to paraphrase Henry David Thoreau, desire to speak like people in a waking moment to other people in their waking moments. But often the poets themselves perform the service of waking us, in a manner like poet Gerard Manley Hopkins who wrote: "The world is charged with the grandeur of God." After encountering a poem such as "God's Grandeur," we are more likely to make an effort to take a closer and more appreciative look at God's world. Poets help us to appreciate that "Everything that is, Is holy." They help us feel more alive and encourage us, by their example, to cleanse our windows of perception in order to see the world anew (both the inner and the outer world) and to enjoy it more abundantly. Thoreau hoped that when he came to the end of his life he could look back on it and know that he had lived "deliberately." The poet Mary Oliver voices a similar sentiment, "When it's over, I want to say: all my life I was a bride married to amazement."[1]

Engaging with Poetry

In giving ourselves over to the reading and then the praying of a poem, we are developing ourselves not only intellectually or aesthetically but also spiritually. Poetry "is a sacred language because it speaks of qualities; and behind qualities, and sustaining them, mysteries, meanings; the holy ground of the soul's country."[2] Thus, surrendering ourselves to reading a poem requires a selflessness akin to prayer. Twentieth-century Jewish mystic Simone Weil defines prayer as "absolute attention" which of its very nature requires selflessness. In that moment of selflessness, she says, God may touch us. Weil's declaration is a daring one, but as we shall see, one based upon her own experience.

In her pivotal essay, "Reflections on the Right Use of School Studies with a View to the Love of God," Weil said:

> Never in any case whatever is a genuine effort of the attention wasted. It always has its effect on the spiritual plane and in consequence on the lower one of the intelligence, for all spiritual light lightens the mind.
>
> If we concentrate our attention on trying to solve a problem of geometry, and if at the end of an hour we are no nearer to doing so than at the beginning, we have nevertheless been making progress each minute of that hour in another more mysterious dimension. Without our knowing or feeling it, this apparently barren effort has brought more light into the soul. The result will one day be discovered in prayer. Moreover, it may very likely be felt in some department of the intelligence in no way connected with mathematics. Perhaps he who made the unsuccessful effort will one day be able to grasp the beauty of a line of Racine more vividly on account of it. But it is cer-

tain that this effort will bear fruit in prayer. There is no doubt whatever about that.[3]

Attention demands the suspension of self-consciousness (the "ego"), for only then are we prepared to be penetrated by the object of our attention. This potentially epiphanic moment occurs anytime we offer our attention to the beauty enshrined in painting, sculpture, music, poetry, or in the beauty of nature. From time immemorial, attention has been one way for all people to lose themselves and to find themselves, reminding us of Christ's words, "In losing yourself, you will find yourself" (cf. Mt 10–39).

When we give ourselves to a close reading and praying of a poem, we are relating to the poem as we would relate to a holy icon. What dynamic occurs when we kneel, sit, or stand before an icon? We gaze at it with complete attention, absorbing its innate beauty and attempting simultaneously to penetrate and to lose ourselves in its mystery. We believe that in some mysterious manner, the icon will aid us in our daily effort to become integrated, spiritual human beings. We understand, perhaps only unconsciously, Plato's dictum, "You become what you behold."

Trappist monk Thomas Merton offers an example of this kind of seeing. After gazing upon Fra Angelico's *Temptation of St. Anthony*, Merton wrote, "Looking at this picture is exactly the same sort of thing as praying."[4] By this Merton does not mean a cursory glance or a museum goer's casual look, but an intense gaze, an act of acute attention that requires a forgetting of the self. In that space between self-consciousness and self-forgetting, where the ego is suspended, there occurs an infinity of transformative and restorative potential.

As masterpieces of art demand intense scrutiny, so does poetry demand close reading if it is to be truly prayed: we, in humility, must surrender ourselves to the poem's beauty and give ourselves totally to understand its meaning. Philosopher and educator John Dewey wrote:

> The work of art operates to deepen and to raise to great clarity that sense of an enveloping undefined whole that accompanies every normal experience. This whole is then felt as an expansion of ourselves. Where egotism is not made the measure of reality and value, we are citizens of this vast world beyond ourselves, and any intense realization of its presence with and in us brings us a peculiar satisfying sense of unity in itself and with ourselves.[5]

Poetry's Power

In times of anxiety, fear, doubt, discouragement and even despair I have gone to the poets, and they have never failed me. Religious poems like Francis Thompson's *The Hound of Heaven* and T. S. Eliot's *Four Quartets* have become for me vibrant mantras of hope and inspiration. The "secular" poetry of Theodore Roethke, John Logan, W. H. Auden and Richard Wilbur also speaks to me, as does the poetry of such converts to Christianity as Thomas Merton, Siegfried Sassoon, Wallace Stevens and Kathleen Raine.

Poets have been where I have been and have transformed their experience into art. Consequently, poets have been gifted with the power to inspire and to guide. Countless people have found a saving word in poetry, a word that offers them the courage to go on, to lift themselves up and to again engage the world. Poet Denise Levertov wrote:

> People turn to poems for some kind of illumination, for revelations that help them to survive, to survive in spirit not only in body. These revelations are usually not of the unheard-of, but of what lies around us unseen or forgotten. Or they illuminate what we feel but don't know we feel until it is articulated.[6]

Never underestimate the power of poetry. I am reminded of the young man in my literature course who came to class every day but rarely participated in our discussions. Sometimes his face was so impassive that I was unsure whether or not he was conscious of what was going on in class. My every effort to engage him fell flat. On the last day of school, he came up to my desk to thank me for a wonderful year. I was stunned. He especially thanked me for the poetry we had studied. He said, "It got me through the year." Later, I discovered that he had attempted to take his life on several occasions during his school tenure, but the poetry we studied had spoken to him. I'll never know how it spoke to him, but it was powerful enough to stay the hand of suicide.

Perhaps for this young man, poetry became prayer. Critic Reed Whittemore notes that Robert Frost discovered the desert places within himself and confronted them by writing a poem. In so doing, poetry "would seem to serve the function of prayer or the confessional, and we, the audience, are moved by the poetry to the extent that it makes a discovery about us too, and then utters our own prayer, makes our confession for us."[7]

Poetry and the Inner Journey

We need poets. From ancient times to the present, poets are people who surrender themselves to the inner journey, and who are indispensable to society because, "…he or she is the explorer, the opener of the way, one who ventures, in a state of inspiration, into regions of consciousness which in most of us remain dark and unexplored."[8]

The source of poetry, therefore, is our deepest inner selves.

The poet becomes our model of being by encouraging us to make an inner journey, although what is often found is disturbing and sometimes disruptive. But the self-knowledge to be gained is at the same time healing and transformative. According to Carl Jung:

> The true genius nearly always intrudes and disturbs. He speaks to a temporal world out of a world eternal. He says the wrong things at the right time. The process of transformation has to make a halt in order to digest, and assimilate the utterly impractical things that the genius has produced from the storehouse of eternity. Yet the genius is the healer

of his time, because anything he reveals of eternal truth is healing.[9]

So when we read a poem, we should be prepared to seek not only an understanding of the poem but a better understanding of ourselves. William Carlos Williams observes that in the act of reading, "The reader knows himself as he was…and he has also in mind a vision of what he would be, some day…. But the thing he never knows and never dares to know is what he is at the exact moment that he is." Poetry opens us to the "now." Of course, what I see in a poem is not what you will see. My enrichment may not be yours. However, truly great poetry is universal; layered in ambiguity, it speaks in many tongues and to many people.

To achieve the kind of attention poetry deserves, we should read it in silence and in solitude. Together silence, solitude, the reader and the poem become a hermitage where God has the opportunity to speak to us through the *lectio divina* of the poet's experience and art. The beauty enshrined in the poem, observed Weil, becomes God's snare. We become God's prey. Thus God captures us by his beauty for he is the source of all beauty.

After reading a poem for the first time, we allow it to sink into us—its rhythm, diction, imagery and meaning. If it is a difficult, obscure poem, we will reflect further. We may then read the poem again. As we are meant to listen carefully to great music over and over again, so too are we meant to reread great poems. In this manner our appreciation expands and deepens. During the time we have focused our attention on the poem, we are lost to the world. In such moments of attention, God may make us aware of his presence or offer us an insight into our own lives, or into life itself. The transformation of epiphany is an ever-present possibility.

The first reading of a poem is like journeying into an unknown land where, like explorers, we may come upon marvels of beauty, insight and radiance that will take our breath away and shake the very foundations of our lives. A person overwhelmed by fear, wrath, lethargy or depression at a poem's beginning may, by its end, turn toward paths of courage, peace, energy or hope. Such is the power of poetry as prayer.

Prayerful Reading

Prayer is often linked with the reading of a prayer book or the Bible. For instance, monastic *lectio divina* revolves around the daily reading of the psalms, perhaps the greatest poems ever written. Every week throughout the world in monasteries and convents, cloistered women and men religious journey through the Psalter. During their community prayer times, they sing the psalms and meditate upon them until the psalms become a part of their being.

Reading other parts of Scripture is also prayer. We may read and then reflect upon a passage until it speaks to us. When we so totally give our attention to reflective prayer, we lose preoccupation with self and enter what T. S. Eliot describes as "the still center of the wheel of time." Upon returning to our ordinary activities, we are often amazed by how much time has passed, for when we immerse ourselves in something other than ourselves, ego and time disappear.

In the art of praying poetry, we give ourselves up to what the mystical poet Raissa Maritain described as "passive absorption."

> Poetry thus appears to me as the fruit of a contact of
> the spirit with reality in itself ineffable, and with its

source which is in truth God himself in the impulse of love which leads him to create images of his beauty.[10]

Poets and saints possess a contemplative nature, and both are disposed to receive intuitions. Poetry, like the mystical prayer of the saints, plunges us into the spiritual depths where there can be a real encounter with the Divine. These are the very hints and guesses that led poets like T. S. Eliot from agnosticism to belief in God, Francis Thompson from the degradation of drug addiction to re-embracing his faith, and G. M. Hopkins to his conversion to Catholicism. Similar intuitions led poet Jessica Powers into a cloistered religious life, Siegfried Sassoon to convert to Catholicism at the end of his life, and Simone Weil to feel that she was possessed by Christ.

Praying poetry, therefore, should never be viewed as trivial as poet Mary Oliver said: "To pay attention: this is our endless and proper work."[11] By this she means attention to the particularity of the natural world. But implicit in her observation is that attention is a discipline we must all bring to our living, or else we take the chance of finding at the end of our lives that we have not lived at all.

Reading a poem attentively and prayerfully is work, as Robert Sardellow wrote:

> Reading is a form of work, of soul work. As such it involves body, mind, soul, spirit…not just the disembodied perceptual apparatus mirroring what presents itself. Every time we read, a secondary making occurs; reading constitutes a part of the creation of the book itself. A book needs a reader in order to be a book. Without a reader, the book is a lifeless object.[12]

Substitute "poem" for "book" and "praying" for "reading" in the above passage, and we better understand the importance and the risk of praying a poem. Risk because we may be transformed from the person we were. I say this not to cause anxiety, but to point out the exciting possibilities poetry extends to all of us.

When Paul Mariani, America's premier biographer of poets, was asked why he had been drawn to poetry, he replied, "Because it gave me hope." A brief and humble answer which points toward the transforming power of great poetry.

Among the poems possessing this exciting opportunity for deep transformation, *The Hound of Heaven* takes pride of place. Based on its author's inner journey, the poem carries us along as one "pilgrim" faces his own darkness and opens himself to the Divine. When prayed, *The Hound of Heaven* has the possibility to reach into our own lives and replace darkness with the Divine.

CHAPTER 2

The Hound of Heaven:
A Spiritual Autobiography

Francis Thompson's ode, *The Hound of Heaven*, is one of the greatest spiritual autobiographies ever written. His three years of destitution on the streets of London and his destructive addiction to laudanum is well known. His subsequent triumph over spiritual, physical and psychological adversity remains one of the most inspirational biographies of all time.

Spiritual autobiographies are an intriguing genre in that they often chronicle a person's flight from and return to God; they are sometimes the narration of spiritual conversion. The greatest ancient autobiography is without doubt Augustine's *Confessions* (c. 400) in which he relates the story of his conversion to Christianity. It is a poignant story, for Augustine resisted God's love for many years by fleeing from it. After thirty years, the prayers of his mother Monica were answered when Augustine finally realized that "Our hearts are restless until they rest in Thee." He was baptized into the Catholic faith, later to become one of the great theologians and saints of the Church.

Cardinal John Henry Newman's *Apologia Pro Vita Sua* (1864) is another riveting autobiography which focuses on England's Oxford Movement and Newman's conversion and reception into the Catholic Church. It is also one of the greatest works ever written in the English language, for Newman was not only a poet but also an elegant prose stylist.

A great modern day autobiography is Thomas Merton's *The Seven Storey Mountain*. Published in 1948, it became a huge bestseller; since then, it has never been out of print. Merton's story is also one of conversion. Like Augustine, Merton fled from the initial movements of God in his soul; he too indulged in a life of sin and ignored the "still, small voice" urging him to offer his life to God. After a fierce struggle with himself, he was baptized into the Catholic faith; he later entered the Cistercian order in Kentucky where he lived the life of an ascetic monk within the cloistered walls of the Abbey of Gethsemani.

Francis Thompson's autobiography differs from the aforementioned in that it is not written in prose but in poetry rich with evocative imagery. While it required

Augustine, Newman and Merton hundreds of pages to tell their story, Thompson narrates his spiritual odyssey in 182 luminous verses.

To use poetry as prayer, and particularly *The Hound of Heaven*, there must be an understanding of the poem's source which is, of course, the poet's life. Francis Thompson's life provides more than enough of the light and shadows needed to create a literary masterpiece, and *The Hound of Heaven* is most fully appreciated when placed within the context of this life of extraordinary illuminations and incredible despair.

Childhood

Francis Thompson was born on December 18, 1859. His parents, physician Charles Thompson and Mary Morton, were converts to the Catholic faith. In fact, before her marriage to Charles Thompson, Francis's mother had briefly attempted religious life. As a boy, Francis was raised in a devout home in Ashton-under-Lyne, near Manchester, England. It was common for Francis to see priests as guests in his parents' home since their Catholic community was a small but close and supportive one.

As a youngster, Francis was an acolyte at his parish; he enjoyed donning the red cassock and surplice and participating in the celebration of the Eucharist. Although legend has it that Francis had always wanted to be a priest, it is unlikely that the legend is true.

At the age of seven Francis exhibited precocious literary leanings, already attempting to read Shakespeare. Thompson relates a charming story regarding his youthful reading habits in a letter:

> When I was a child of seven, standing in my nightgown before the fire, and chattering to my mother, I remember her pulling me up for using a certain word. "That is not used nowadays," she said, "that is one of Shakespeare's words." "Is it, Mamma," I said, staring at her doubtfully. "But I didn't know it was one of Shakespeare's words!" "That is just it," she answered "you have read Shakespeare so much that you are beginning to talk Shakespeare without knowing it. You must take care or people will think you odd." She was a prophetess.[1]

College

At the age of eleven, Francis entered St. Cuthbert's College, Ushaw, a Catholic school well known for preparing boys for the priesthood. It soon became clear to the priests, however, that Francis was not suited for the priesthood. He was too dreamy and possessed a certain "indolence" that precluded religious life. This was a great disappointment to Thompson's parents, especially his father, who then decided that Francis would become a doctor. In 1877, at the age of seventeen, Francis enrolled at Owens Medical College, Manchester, where for six years he unsuccessfully studied medicine.

Later, after Thompson had become famous as a poet, his father lamented, "Why didn't he tell me he wanted to be a poet?" Indeed, Thompson's dominant trait as a young man was reticence. He could have avoided much heartache both for himself and his loving parents if he had only told them that he really wanted to be a poet. But he never opposed his father and obediently attended first the seminary and then medical school.

We can easily understand such actions; many children wish to make their parents happy and often will enter professions for which they are unsuited. They delude themselves into believing that they are doing so out of love, when in fact it is simply a fear of offending their parents and of asserting their autonomy as adults. Francis once admitted that he really never wanted to grow up, which may explain this childlike attitude of submission.

Addiction

It is conjectured that Thompson acquired his addiction to laudanum (alcohol with a tincture of opium) at the age of 20 when he was attending Owens Medical College. Prior to entering Owens, Francis's mother had given him a birthday gift of *Confessions of an Opium Eater* by the author Thomas De Quincey. Little did she realize how De Quincey's magical, mesmerizing prose descriptions of his opium-induced visions would dazzle her impressionable son. Thompson once remarked, "Shelley is my polestar in poetry, De Quincey in prose." It seems De Quincey also became a role model for the budding poet. We can rightly wonder what may have happened to Thompson if his mother had gifted him with Augustine's *Confessions* rather than De Quincey's *Confessions*.

At Owens, Thompson attended class regularly but failed his medical finals three times. He obviously never should have entertained the idea of becoming a doctor, later admitting that the very sight of blood made him faint. His father was sorely disappointed by his son's failure to secure a profession with which to support himself. He later managed to procure Francis a job selling surgical supplies. Failing at that too, Francis tried to sell encyclopedias, but he read the complete set without selling one. His final attempt at a profession was to enlist in the army, but he was quickly found lacking in will and in stamina.

On November 8, 1885, Thompson and his father engaged in an emotionally charged argument. The cause of the dispute has been much debated. Dr. Thompson may have accused his son of drinking excessively, unaware that his son was already deeply involved in addiction. Or Dr. Thompson may have discovered laudanum, a common medicinal pain-killer found in most doctor's offices, missing from his own supplies, and suspected his son's pilfering. Whatever the reason, Francis departed for London with nothing but two books, a poetry volume of William Blake in one pocket and Greek poet and dramatist Aeschylus in the other.

Life on London's Streets

In London, Francis, an educated and articulate young man, easily found employment with a bookseller. But his salary was quickly invested in his laudanum habit, and he lost his job when he became incapable of performing the simplest duties. He eventually joined the thousands of homeless living in the London streets. Emulating other downtrodden men, he earned money selling matches or pencils, boot-blacking or holding horses. Without lodging, he slept along the Thames embankment near Victoria Station or in one of London's parks or under the arches of the cities' many bridges.

Destitute, Thompson was walking down a street near Leicester Square one day when a man greeted him, "Is your soul saved?" Affronted, Thompson challenged his questioner, "What right have you to ask me that?" The man was Mr. McMaster, an owner of a boot shop and a zealous Evangelical. He was known to rescue the poor and lowly from the city's streets, and to restore them to respectability. He became friendly with Thompson, offering him lodging and employment. It is likely that during the calm days with McMaster, Thompson began writing his essay "Paganism Old and New," the work that would soon establish his literary reputation. During this time Thompson valiantly tried to conquer his drug habit, but was unsuccessful. Gradually his addiction became so extreme that his benefactor was forced to ask him to leave. Years later, after Thompson had become a famous poet, McMaster admitted that Thompson was his only failure.

Back again on the streets and miserable, Thompson despaired and decided to take his own life. With his last bit of money he purchased a large quantity of laudanum and headed for the rear of Covent Garden, where the daily rubbish of the market place was piled high. That he would choose such a place to end his life eloquently illustrates his psychological state. He had imbibed half the bottle of laudanum when he felt a hand encircling his wrist, preventing him from drinking the second, certainly fatal dose. Thompson believed it to be the hand of the deceased teenage poet, Thomas Chatterton. Legend says that Chatterton had taken his own life, unaware that rescue in the form of money was on its way to him. It arrived the day after his suicide. Thompson was shaken by this inner vision and decided to endure a while longer.

A Woman's Pity

Soon after this a young woman took pity on the sickly Thompson who was already suffering from tuberculosis. She saw him shivering in the arches of Covent Garden when she invited him to reside with her until he regained his health. We do not know her name, but Thompson described her as a prostitute. Whether or not Thompson's relationship with her was more than platonic, we may never know for certain. But he always spoke lovingly of her and immortalized her in a sonnet published posthumously:

> Who clasp lost spirits, also clasp their hell;
> > You have clasped, and burn, sad child, sad
> > > Semele!
> One half of my cup have you drunk too well,

And that's the death; the immortality
 Girt in the fiery spirit flies your lip.
You should be mother, bear your fellowship
 I' the mortal grief, without the immortal gain!
Not only I, that these poor verses live,
 A heavy vigil keep of parched nights;
  But you for unborn men your pangs must
   give,
And wake in tears that they may dream delights.
What poems be, Sweet, you did never know;
 And yet are poems suckled by your woe![2]

It should be stated here that years later, after Thompson had recovered enough to begin a new life, he went in search of this woman who had saved him from certain death on the mist-shrouded London streets. But he was never able to find her. Perhaps she knew that their relationship would never be understood or accepted; thus, she disappeared forever.

Hope for the Struggling Poet

When he was lodging with this woman, Thompson completed his essay "Paganism Old and New" and mailed it along with a few poems to the monthly magazine *Merry England*, edited by Wilfrid Meynell. Thompson wrote:

Dear Sir,

In enclosing the accompanying article for your inspection, I must ask pardon for the soiled state of the manuscript. It is due, not to slovenliness, but to the strange places and circumstances under which it has been written. For me, no less than Parolles, the dirty nurse Experience has something fouled. I enclose a stamped envelope for a reply; since I do not desire the return of the manuscript, regarding your judgment of its worthlessness as quite final. I can hardly expect that where my prose fails my verse will succeed. Nevertheless, on the principle of "yet will I try the last," I have added a few specimens of it, with the off-chance that one may be less poor than the rest. Apologizing very sincerely for my intrusion on your valuable time, I remain,

Yours with little hope,
Francis Thompson

Kindly address your rejection to the Charring Cross Post Office.

Meynell pigeonholed the soiled manuscript and letter for six months before noticing it again. Then, as he was burning the rejected writings which had accumulated in his office over several months, Meynell discovered the bundle, and began to read Thompson's essay and poems

He was instantly astounded by the author's erudition and poetic flair and unsuccessfully tried to contact Thompson for permission to publish. Failing to find him, he decided to proceed with publication of the poem "Passion of Mary," in the hope that its author would contact him. Thompson did through a letter.

Dear Sir,

In the last days of February or the first days of March 1877, (my memory fails me as to the exact date) I forwarded to you for your magazine a prose article, ("Paganism, Old & New," or "Ancient & Modern," for I forget which wording I adopted) and accompanied it by some pieces of verse, on the chance that if the prose failed, some of the verse might meet acceptance....

To be brief, from that day to this, no answer has ever come into my hands. And yet, more than a twelve month since the forwarding of the manuscript, I am now informed that one of the copies of verse which I submitted to you (i.e. "The Passion of Mary") is appearing in this month's issue of *Merry England.*

I therefore enclose a stamped and addressed envelope for an answer, hoping that you will recompense me for my long delay by the favour of an early reply. In any case, however, long circumstances may possibly delay your reply, it will be sure of reaching me at the address I have now given.

> I remain,
> Yours respectfully,
> Francis Joseph Thompson

A Lifelong Friendship

We now come to one of the most poignant events in the life of the poet Francis Thompson: The meeting between the poet and Wilfrid Meynell.

Meynell had been alone in his office when he received a visitor. "I was at work when the door opened. A shadow of a figure half-appeared, and the door shut again. The door was opened again, with somebody hesitating to enter, and was shut again. I got up, opened it, and there was Thompson, frightened to come in."[3]

We can only imagine the terror Francis Thompson experienced. How much courage it must have cost him to arrive at the *Merry England* office, dressed in rags, poorer looking than the average beggar, with no shirt beneath his coat and bare feet in broken shoes and to stand before the impeccably dressed Victorian gentleman and editor Wilfrid Meynell. But Meynell was a kind and compassionate man; disregarding appearances his eyes penetrated to the man beneath the rags. "You must have had access to many books when you wrote that essay." Thompson's humble reply was "That is precisely where the essay fails. I had no books by me at the time, save Aeschylus and Blake." Thus begins one of the great friendships of all time. Wilfrid Meynell became confidant, brother and father to the poet who went on to write some of the most memorable English verse ever composed.

At the time of their first meeting, Thompson's health was near total collapse and Meynell wisely admitted him to a private hospital where he underwent laudanum withdrawal. After six weeks of recuperation the poet was moved to lodgings not far from Meynell's home, and was employed as a book reviewer by Meynell's Catholic magazine *Merry England*. This kind of work exhibited Thompson's astonishing literary erudition, and Meynell was delighted with his "find." However, he had no idea yet that the young man he rescued from the London streets was also a poetic genius. Proof of that would come later.

Monastery Days
At the beginning of the new year, 1889, Thompson succumbed again to his addiction. To save him from the

temptations that abounded in the London streets, Meynell arranged for Thompson to retire to a monastery in Sussex where he could take in the fresh air and the monastic silence and solitude which would surely restore him to health. The monastery was that of the Canons of Premontre in the village of Storrington. It was a French order, but this presented no problem for Thompson who was fluent in the language.

By May 1889 Thompson saw light at the end of the tunnel of his agonizing addiction withdrawal. One evening, as he so often did, Thompson paused in a priory-owned field. Before his eyes, the setting sun transformed the sky into an artist's palette of multicolored hues. As he stood near the priory's life-size crucifix in the field, he heard the music of three itinerant musicians who were passing by.

We can imagine the poet gazing at the setting sun and contemplating his own life: his suffering, his humiliations, his youth wasted upon the loathsome London streets, and his debilitating addiction to laudanum. Now it was spring; all of nature had been reborn before him in the beauty of the Sussex countryside where the poet's wounded soul had found refuge and strength. He felt his own rebirth within his soul: the rebirth of his poetical gifts, but more important the rebirth of his relationship with Christ. In the beauty of the setting sun with its promise of rebirth on the morrow, he saw a symbol of Christ's death and resurrection.

When the sun emerged from veiling clouds, a single ray of light shone upon Christ's crucified body. In an instant of illumination, the poet perceived in the cross the mystical symbol par excellence, one resonating with all that Thompson whole-heartedly believed, with all that he had lived and with all that he had hoped for. He realized that Christ upon the cross is the light of the world, the Alpha and the Omega. He wrote:

Thy straight
    Long beam lies steady on the Cross. Ah me!
What secret would thy radiant finger show?
    Of thy bright mastership is this the key?
Is this the secret, then? And is it the woe? [4]

As a Catholic, Thompson had already known the answer to his question: Love is the secret. Christ died for us because he loves us forever in the Eternal Now, and as the mystic Julian of Norwich reminds us, he would die for us over and over again so endless is his love for us. But the Cross always involves suffering; perhaps it is this that

Thompson had fled from, afraid to pick up and carry his own cross, avoiding it in a drug-induced dream world.

How fitting that under the great corpus of Jesus' body on the cross, Thompson was inspired to write what many critics consider an ode equal to *The Hound of Heaven: The Ode to the Setting Sun.* When Thompson completed his *Ode,* he sent it to Wilfrid Meynell and to Meynell's wife Alice, herself an accomplished and respected poet. Both were astonished by the splendor of the verse, its structure, its profound theology, its imagery and beauty. Now they knew for certain that they had assisted in the regeneration of a poet obviously destined for greatness. They immediately set out for Storrington to meet with the poet, to celebrate his spiritual rebirth and the creation of his magnificent ode. Later the poem was published in *Merry England* with this brief preface from Wilfrid Meynell, "Its appearance is nothing less than an event in the annals of English poetry."

We unfortunately do not have the diary Thompson kept during his thirteen months at Storrington. Thompson's biographer John Walsh had searched for it in the Priory at Storrington and in the Canons' central house in Avignon, France, but to no avail. It must have been a remarkable document: an insightful and inspiring spiritual testament. That a man near death could so turn his life around is a story whose details could only be inspiring and life-giving to readers, especially to those easily discouraged by the slightest setback.

Besides *The Ode to the Setting Sun*, another noticeable indication of Thompson's return to health was his friendliness with Storrington's rural children who daily passed by the monastery on their way to school. They were not in the least frightened by the eccentric man in the scuffed boots and shabby overcoat, worn even on the warmest of days. Thompson possessed a rare spiritual affinity for children, himself being unpretentious and childlike. One child in particular, Daisy, became the poet's friend. Remembering a day picking wild raspberries with Thompson, she said, "He helped me fill my basket and any extra fine one I found I'd give him to eat." This meeting with Daisy resulted in a poem critics compare to Wordsworth's "Lucy" poems:

> She looked a little wistfully,
> Then went her sunshine way:—
> The sea's eye had a mist on it
> And the leaves fell from the day.
>
> She went her unremembering way,

She went and left in me
The pang of all the partings gone,
And partings yet to be.

    She left me marveling why my soul
Was sad that she was glad;
At all the sadness in the sweet,
The sweetness in the sad.

    Still, still I seemed to see her, still
Look up with soft replies,
And take the berries with her hand
And the love with her lovely eyes.

    Nothing begins, and nothing ends,
That is not paid with moan;
For we are born in other's pain,
And perish in our own.[5]

During his stay at Storrington Thompson began composing his most famous ode, *The Hound of Heaven*. Thompson's diary would surely have thrown light on the inspiration for this splendid ode, but we are left to speculate about its actual source and gestation. We do know, however, that from the initial stages of the poem's composition, Thompson himself knew it was extraordinary, the fruit of his own genius. He wrote in his notebook:

At this time visited me the rudimentary conception of *The Hound of Heaven*—certainly with all its shortcomings, the greatest of my odes: and this because it embodies a world-wide experience in an individual form of that experience: the universal becoming incarnated in the personal. It was a very rudimentary conception with nothing like the scope it later took to itself, but I felt it great In suggestion— too great for my present powers of execution. Fortunately I shrank from executing it: and when I ultimately encountered it again I was much like the fisherman who freed the "ginn" from his vessel.[6]

From the same notebook, we learn that during this time Thompson came to consider Wordsworth the poet of the Return to Nature and himself the poet of the Return to God.

A New Life

After regaining his physical health at Storrington, Thompson returned to London. Although monasteries located in rural areas of Great Britain became Thompson's sanctuaries during times of illness, the poet always returned to London after his physical and psychological health had improved. Thompson had always been an urban person; he knew that if he were to make a name for himself as a poet, he would have to do so in London, the center of literary life at that time. He had understood this when he left his father's home in his mid-twenties to follow his literary dream.

Furthermore, he could not continue to rely on the kindness of monks; he needed a home. Perhaps in his heart he longed to be married, to have children, to live the kind of ordered, enriching existence the Meynells maintained so well with their large family and even larger circle of friends. Although Thompson twice fell in love, he was temperamentally unsuited for a wife and family, in part because he had irreparably damaged his body during his laudanum addiction, a habit he never truly conquered. Even after he acquired fame as a poet, he suffered relapses up to the time of his death.

However, when departing from Storrington, Thompson was a confident man. He had proven to the Meynells that he was indeed a poet with the splendor of *The Ode to the Setting Sun,* and his first draft of *The Hound of Heaven.*

In 1890 Thompson took residence in Queen's Park, London, not far from the Meynells' home at Palace Court. Employed again by Wilfred Meynell, Thompson became a competent contributor to *Merry England* as well as the

Register, doing editorial work and writing for both Catholic publications.

Thompson's three books were all published in the 1890s: *Poems,* which included *The Hound of Heaven,* in 1893; *Sister Songs* in 1895; and *New Poems* in 1897. Neither the second nor the third volume was as successful as the first.

During the years he was enjoying acclaim as a poet, Thompson continued struggling with his opium addiction. Twice the Meynells arranged for Thompson to move to accommodations near a monastery, hoping that the influence of the monastic lifestyle would again help to pull Thompson out of his addiction and return him to health.

Unfortunately, any recovery that Thompson enjoyed was short-lived. In the late 1890s, he reverted to regular opium use, and his health began to decline at an alarming rate. The years between 1890 and 1907 were years of immense struggle for the poet. On November 13, 1907, Francis Thompson died, and his biographer John Walsh noted, "Exact cause of death, whether from drugs or tuberculosis, remains in doubt."

CHAPTER 3

The Hound of Heaven: Mystical Literature

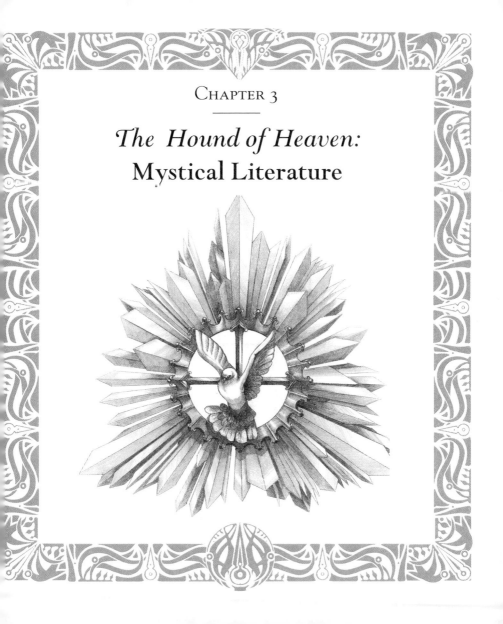

Voices of Praise

Because Francis Thompson's first book *Poems* received skillful prepublication marketing by Wilfrid Meynell, the book of verse was widely reviewed, and the poem that reviewers concentrated on was *The Hound of Heaven*. At first the poem received mixed reviews. But its fame began with comments such as that of the poet Coventry Patmore:

> *The Hound of Heaven* has so great and passionate, such a meter-creating motive, that we are carried over all obstructions of the rhythmical current, and are compelled to pronounce it, at the end, one of the few "great" odes of which the language can boast.[1]

In *The Bookman*, Katharine Tynan wrote:

To read Mr. Francis Thompson's poems is like setting sail with Drake or Hawkins in search of new worlds and golden spoils. He has the magnificent Elizabethan manner, the splendour of conception, the largeness of imagery.[2]

Gilbert Keith Chesterton wrote in the *Illustrated London News:*

In Francis Thompson's poetry, as in the poetry of the universe, you can work infinitely out and out, and yet infinitely in and in. These two infinities are the mark of greatness.[3]

Mr. J. L. Garvin, in the *Newcastle Chronicle,* wrote:

We don't think we forget any of the splendid things of an English anthology when we say that *The Hound of Heaven* seems to us, on the whole, the most wonderful lyric in the language. It fingers all the stops of the spirit, and we have now a thrilling and dolorous note of doom, and now the quiring of the spheres, and now the very pipes of Pan, but under all the still, sad music of humanity.[4]

Overnight Thompson became a celebrity not only because he was a new, exciting poetic voice, but also because his life on the London streets fascinated the verse-reading world. His poetry became popular in France and especially in Catholic Ireland where priest and author Father Sheehan praised the poem as if it had originated in his own land, "the nation of eternity." William Butler Yeats said of the poem, "*The Hound of Heaven* leaps but into empty hearts." Readers in search of spiritual sustenance were especially drawn to Thompson's verse. We are told that even Oscar Wilde was quite moved when he heard Thompson's poem read to him; he is said to have remarked, "That is the poetry I have always wanted to write."

In our own day poet James Dickey is eloquent regarding *The Hound of Heaven*:

> The "Hound" (and who but a man of Thompson's peculiar baroque-mystic orientation would have used this as the figure of God?) pursues simply by being the creator of and in-dweller in everything that is, imbuing all things with His essential quality of love. His gentle pursuit seems the most dreadful possible one to the sinner desperate to keep his youth and powers intact. However, it takes on something of the truly ominous—pursuit, itself, is terrifying—and there is something particularly terrible in the conviction that grows in both sinner and reader that there is literally no escape. Thompson has entered, as well as created, his vision of the sinner-as-quarry, and turned the cosmos into a ritual hunt in some of

the most frankly gorgeous imagery, some of the most resounding and yet curiously individual rhetoric, since Milton.[5]

Bishop Fulton J. Sheen, author and television personality, wrote:

> One of the most beautiful descriptions of God in pursuit of the soul is that of Francis Thompson in the poem, *The Hound of Heaven*. The "Hound" is God, rapid in his pursuit, and there is nothing new in such a name for him. Sophocles, in one of his dramas, speaks of "Heaven's Winged Hound," just as a Punic inscription speaks of "Kelbilim," the Hound of Divinity.[6]

It is remarkable that a religious poem written by a Catholic would receive such attention in late nineteenth-century England, that Anglicans memorized it and young Etonians studied it. Of course, the 1833 beginning of the Oxford Movement, along with John Henry Newman's conversion to Catholicism, had put religion very much in the forefront of English life. A number of Oxford's intellectuals had converted to Catholicism, including the brilliant Gerard Manley Hopkins whose poetry was as "strange" as that of Thompson's. Interestingly, Hopkins's verses were not published until 1918. How different the world of poetry in England might have been had both Hopkins and Thompson arisen upon the poetic landscape at the same time: perhaps a more wide-spread and permanent English Catholic revival.

Themes in *The Hound of Heaven*

The Hound of Heaven is a daring poem fraught with highly charged symbols chronicling the age-old theme of God's perpetual pursuit of souls. In fact, the poem can be read as a paradigm of soul-making, one well documented in the mystical literature of Western Christianity.

How had Thompson latched onto the concept of the Hound as an image of God in pursuit of the soul? We are not sure, despite the fact that employing an animal as a metaphor for the Divine is not rare. Throughout the world at the Eucharistic Celebration, we recite the *Agnus Dei*, "Lamb of God you who take away the sins of the world, have mercy on us." Only a few years before Thompson, Gerard Manley Hopkins had compared Christ to a soaring falcon in his great poem *The Windhover*. The exact inspiration for Thompson arriving at this metaphor for God remains unclear; nevertheless, it has captured the imagination of countless men and women.

The theme of flight from God, however, is easier to comprehend, because flight from God is a dominant theme of Scripture. The ode beautifully echoes Psalm 138: "Where shall I go from your spirit? Where shall I flee from your face?" It also echoes Augustine, who poetically narrates his own flight from the Divine:

> Late have I loved Thee, O Beauty, so ancient and so new; late have I loved Thee! For behold Thou wert within me, and I outside; and I sought Thee outside and in my unloveliness fell upon those lovely things that Thou hast made. Thou wert with me and I was not with Thee. I was kept from Thee by these things, yet had they not been in Thee, they could not have been at all. Thou didst call and cry to me and break open my deafness: and Thou didst send forth Thy beams and shine upon me and chase away my blindness…. Thou didst touch me, and I have burned for Thy peace.[7]

In recent years, Thompson's poetry has undergone reappraisal, for his verse still speaks in myriad ways to the modern reader. We may instantly recognize that Thompson's experience of Church was that of the late nineteenth century, but this should not discourage us. Readers can still be refreshed in the pure springs of his verse. Do we not continue to read Shakespeare even though the externals of his world and his language have drastically changed? We read him because we are not so much interested in social customs or manners as we are interested in the universality (or catholicism, if you will) of his art. The litmus test of every encounter with great art is: Does it speak to the human condition? Surely, in the case of Francis Thompson's poetry, the answer is yes.

For those who have the eyes to see and the ears to hear, there is enough meditation material in *The Hound of Heaven* to last a lifetime. Thompson is so very human, notably human among the world's poets. The brilliant young man who had failed to find his path in life until it was almost too late went on to create verse that eloquently speaks to us today of the inner life. If we but listen, we will be immeasurably enriched. One critic observes:

> Many good judges are prepared to call Thompson the greatest mystical poet of the English tongue; and it is certainly no easy task to name any writer of mystical verse who surpasses him in his combination of ardent devotion, splendid imagination and sumptuous diction.[8]

The beauty alone of *The Hound of Heaven*, which Thompson's biographer John Walsh describes as the "foremost religious poem of modern times," demands attention from discerning readers. Poet and author Louis Untermeyer says the poem "moves with the unhurried majesty of a Bach Chorale, building verse upon fugal verse into unterrestrial architecture…with an almost divine excess."[9]

There is enough dramatic, spiritual and psychological profundity to justify a great deal of time spent with *The Hound of Heaven*. The same may be said of Thompson's other works, especially his *Ode to the Setting Sun* and *The Kingdom of Heaven*, or the simpler lyrics like *The Poppy* and *Daisy* and the exquisite *To a Snowflake*. These poems equal those of other eminent Victorian poets such as Tennyson, Browning and Arnold. Comparison of Thompson's poetry to that of the Gerard Manley Hopkins proves the worth of both men, who chronicle the beauty of God's world and the terror of life without him.

Naturally, Thompson's poetry has been most often interpreted in the Catholic mystical tradition. It is not unusual to see Thompson's name mentioned in the company of mystics like Julian of Norwich, Ignatius of Loyola,

John of the Cross and Teresa of Avila. But he is also numbered among great English poets: Richard Crashaw, George Herbert, John Donne, Henry Vaughn, William Wordsworth, and Coventry Patmore.

The time is also ripe to read Thompson from the perspective of modern psychology. Because Thompson's poetry is fraught with archetypal imagery, a Jungian interpretation of his verse would surely yield fresh insights, bringing his experiences closer to today's readers. The title of Carl Jung's *Modern Man in Search of a Soul* suggests that perhaps Thompson's poem is not only about God's search for him, but also God's search for each of us today.

Thompson is the very poet so many of us need in today's world, and *The Hound of Heaven* as a prayer-poem speaks to the deepest longings of our spirits. With open mind and heart let us now turn our gaze to this mystical poem.

Chapter 4

The Hound of Heaven

I fled Him, down the nights and down the days;
   I fled Him, down the arches of the years;
I fled Him, down the labyrinthine ways
   Of my own mind; and in the mist of tears
I hid from Him, and under running laughter.
         Up vistaed hopes I sped;
         And shot, precipitated,
Adown Titanic glooms of chasmèd fears,
   From those strong Feet that followed, followed after.
       But with unhurrying chase,
       And unperturbèd pace,
     Deliberate speed, majestic instancy,
       They beat—and a Voice beat
       More instant than the Feet—
"All things betray thee, who betrayest Me."

I pleaded, outlaw-wise,
By many a hearted casement, curtained red,
   Trellised with intertwining charities;
(For, though I knew His love Who followèd,
            Yet was I sore adread
Lest, having Him, I must have naught beside);
But, if one little casement parted wide,
   The gust of His approach would clash it to.
   Fear wist not to evade, as Love wist to pursue.
Across the margent of the world I fled,
   And troubled the gold gateways of the stars,
   Smiting for shelter on their clangèd bars;
            Fretted to dulcet jars
And silvern chatter the pale ports o' the moon.
I said to Dawn: Be sudden—to Eve: Be soon;
   With thy young skiey blossoms heap me over
            From this tremendous Lover—
Float thy vague veil about me, lest He see!
   I tempted all His servitors, but to find
My own betrayal in their constancy,
In faith to Him their fickleness to me,
   Their traitorous trueness, and their loyal deceit.
To all swift things for swiftness did I sue;
   Clung to the whistling mane of every wind.

But whether they swept, smoothly fleet,
The long savannahs of the blue;
Or whether, Thunder-driven,
They clanged His chariot 'thwart a heaven
Plashy with flying lightnings round the spurn o' their
feet:—
Fear wist not to evade as Love wist to pursue.
Still with unhurrying chase,
And unperturbèd pace,
Deliberate speed, majestic instancy,
Came on the following Feet,
And a Voice above their beat—
"Naught shelters thee, who wilt not shelter Me."

I sought no more that after which I strayed
In face of man or maid;
But still within the little children's eyes
Seems something, something that replies,
They at least are for me, surely for me!
I turned me to them very wistfully;
But just as their young eyes grew sudden fair
With dawning answers there,
Their angel plucked them from me by the hair.

"Come then, ye other children, Nature's—share
With me" (said I) "your delicate fellowship;
    Let me greet you lip to lip,
    Let me twine you with caresses,
        Wantoning
    With our Lady-Mother's vagrant tresses,
        Banqueting
    With her in her wind-walled palace,
    Underneath her azured daïs,
    Quaffing, as your taintless way is,
        From a chalice
Lucent-weeping out of the dayspring."
        So it was done:
I in their delicate fellowship was one—
Drew the bolt of Nature's secrecies.
    I knew all the swift importings
    On the wilful face of skies;
    I knew how the clouds arise
    Spumèd of the wild sea-snortings;
        All that's born or dies
    Rose and drooped with; made them shapers
Of mine own moods, or wailful or divine;
    With them joyed and was bereaven.

I was heavy with the even,
When she lit her glimmering tapers
Round the day's dead sanctities.
I laughed in the morning's eyes.
I triumphed and I saddened with all weather,
Heaven and I wept together,
And its sweet tears were salt with mortal mine.
Against the red throb of its sunset-heart
I laid my own to beat,
And share commingling heat;
But not by that, by that, was eased my human smart.
In vain my tears were wet on Heaven's grey cheek.
For ah! we know not what each other says,
These things and I; in sound *I* speak—
Their sound is but their stir, they speak by silences,
Nature, poor stepdame, cannot slake my drouth;
Let her, if she would owe me,
Drop yon blue bosom-veil of sky, and show me
The breasts o' her tenderness:
Never did any milk of hers once bless
My thirsting mouth.
Nigh and nigh draws the chase,
With unperturbèd pace,
Deliberate speed, majestic instancy;

And past those noisèd Feet
A Voice comes yet more fleet—
"Lo naught contents thee, who content'st not
Me."

Naked I wait Thy love's uplifted stroke!
My harness piece by piece Thou has hewn from me,
And smitten me to my knee;
I am defenceless utterly.
I slept, methinks, and woke,
And, slowly gazing, find me stripped in sleep.
In the rash lustihead of my young powers,
I shook the pillaring hours
And pulled my life upon me; grimed with smears,
I stand amid the dust o' the mounded years—
My mangled youth lies dead beneath the heap,
My days have crackled and gone up in smoke,
Have puffed and burst as sun-starts on a stream.
Yea, faileth now even dream
The dreamer, and the lute the lutanist;
Even the linked fantasies, in whose blossomy twist
I swung the earth a trinket at my wrist,
Are yielding; cords of all too weak account
For earth with heavy griefs so overplussed.

Ah! is Thy love indeed
A weed, albeit an amaranthine weed,
Suffering no flowers except its own to mount?
          Ah! must—
          Designer infinite!—
Ah! must Thou char the wood ere Thou canst limn
     with it?
My freshness spent its wavering shower i' the dust;
And now my heart is as a broken fount,
Wherein tear-drippings stagnate, spilt down ever
          From the dank thoughts that shiver
Upon the sighful branches of my mind.
          Such is; what is to be?
The pulp so bitter, how shall taste the rind?
I dimly guess what Time in mists confounds;
Yet ever and anon a trumpet sounds
From the hid battlements of Eternity;
Those shaken mists a space unsettle, then
Round the half-glimpsèd turrets slowly wash again.
          But not ere him who summoneth
          I first have seen, enwound
With glooming robes purpureal, cypress-crowned;
His name I know, and what his trumpet saith.

Whether man's heart or life it be which yields
     Thee harvest, must Thy harvest-fields
     Be dunged with rotten death?

      Now of that long pursuit
      Comes on at hand the bruit;
    That Voice is round me like a bursting sea:
      "And is thy earth so marred,
      Shattered in shard on shard?
    Lo, all things fly thee, for thou fliest Me!
    Strange, piteous, futile thing!
Wherefore should any set thee love apart?
Seeing none but I make much of naught" (He said),
"And human love needs human meriting:
     How hast thou merited—
Of all man's clotted clay the dingiest clot?
     Alack, thou knowest not
How little worthy of any love thou art!
Whom wilt thou find to love ignoble thee,
     Save Me, save only Me?
All which I took from thee I did but take,
     Not for thy harms,
But just that thou might'st seek it in My arms.

All which thy child's mistake
Fancies as lost, I have stored for thee at home:
　　Rise, clasp My hand, and come!"

　Halts by me that footfall:
　Is my gloom, after all,
Shade of His hand, outstretched carressingly?
　"Ah, fondest, blindest, weakest,
　I am He whom thou seekest!
Thou dravest love from thee, who dravest Me."

CHAPTER 5

The Hound of Heaven: A Meditation

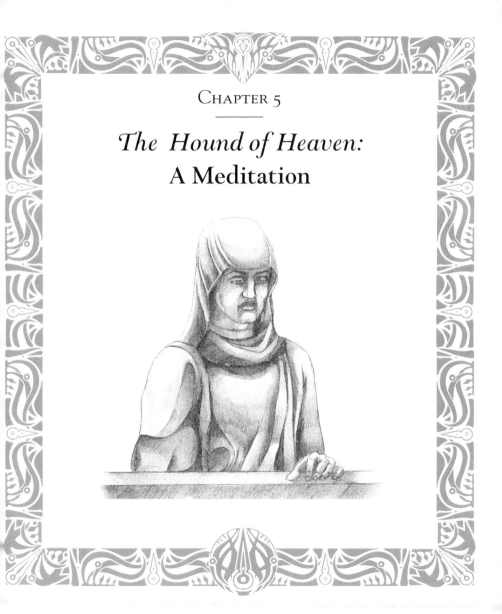

I fled Him,

The poet immediately confesses his lifelong spiritual flight from God. Employing the past tense verb "fled," the speaker offers a retrospective view of his life, a narrative technique used masterfully by Augustine in his autobiography *Confessions*. Like the great saint, the poet Francis Thompson also speaks from his heart to our hearts about his past, with courage and humility.

The first three words swiftly draw us into the poet's inner life; his verse serves as a mirror in which we see ourselves. Thompson, like all Christians, is a pilgrim on earth where his purpose is to know, love and serve God. We, too, know what it is to flee from God, to sin, to be ignorant, and to be weak. In this first verse we intuit that here is the story of a soul, one filled with darkness, loneliness, emptiness and anguish. We also understand its catholicism, its universality; we understand that in reading the poet's verse, we are reading our own life's story

"I fled Him." The first word of this lengthy poem is *I*—the first person singular pronoun representing the ego. I choose myself over God. In fact, in my choice I decide to turn my back on God and to flee from him. Is not this choice the root of all sin, all estrangement, all alienation, all unhappiness?

Thompson's flight from God was likely exacerbated by his addiction. Thompson must have known that opium possessed the potential to impair if not completely destroy him both spiritually and physically. He knew of two poets whose powers were greatly diminished by addiction. Besides Thomas De Quincey's story, Thompson also knew of the extent to which opium had permanently impaired the poetical gifts of Samuel Taylor Coleridge, who never fulfilled his genius as he imbibed a half pint of laudanum every day for much of his adult life.

As a Catholic, Francis Thompson probably understood the idea of an "occasion of sin." Yet, he put himself in danger by seeking out the life-destroying drug; thus, he endangered not only his genius and physical health, but more importantly he endangered his spiritual health.

Perhaps we should think about those "addictions" in our lives which keep us from being whole human beings, those practices or habits which prevent us from being holy and spiritually healthy. Perhaps we should ask ourselves: "What am I running away from?" The Trappist monk Thomas Merton profoundly understood the results of flight from God. After years spent in silence, solitude and prayer, he learned that to maintain a meaningful, intimate relationship with God, he had to be completely honest with himself because the contemplation of God demands truth and courage.

T. S. Eliot observes, "Humankind cannot bear much reality." To face reality is difficult, yes, but not impossible. With grace we can face God and not flee from him. It is our choice to say "yes" or "no" to God's grace.

down the nights and down the days;

The soul flees from God "down the nights and down the days" which means always. During the night and the day. During the sunrise times of life and the times of sunset. During the days of consciousness, the nights of sleep, the days of health and the nights of ill health, the days of joy and the nights of sorrow; during the days free of addiction and the nights lost in the opium haze of hallucinations. But no matter where the soul flees, no matter what time of day or year it is, God is present.

I fled Him, down the arches of the years;

In London, Thompson daily viewed the arches of bridges crossing the Thames; many a night he slept on the Thames embankment. In severe rain and snow, he sought shelter beneath these arches as do many of London's homeless today. Perhaps Thompson imagined himself fleeing from God under a succession of arches because he spent so many lonely, opium-haunted nights beneath such half-circles, enveloped in the murky mist rising from the Thames, huddled with other poverty-stricken men, women and children.

An arch is a support, a construction that upholds a great weight, and is often seen in religious buildings, such as the stone arches of medieval monasteries or great cathedrals like Notre Dame. God is our arch; he supports us always. We often think, in our self-centeredness, that we have endured a difficulty alone, or upheld ourselves through an illness or emotional turmoil, but it is really God holding us up.

God is closer to us than we are to ourselves. The arch is a half circle, and when we surrender to God's love, we complete the circle; only in such manner do we become whole and holy.

I fled Him, down the labyrinthine ways
  Of my own mind;

These verses are perhaps the most well-known of *The Hound of Heaven*. The image of the maze intrigues people because it is such a resonant metaphor for modern life. Who of us has not become lost in the maze of today's confusion, anxiety, and fear? Why do we run away from him who loves us more than we love ourselves, who is closer to us than we are to ourselves?

Children sometimes enjoy entering a maze of shrubbery, to see if they can find their way out. Sometimes they panic, feeling totally lost, and wail until their parents quicken to the rescue to lead them from the confusing and frightening maze, comforting them.

How often as adults we lose ourselves in a maze of anxiety. Grown now, we cannot depend on our parents to rescue us, but God is always present and ready to lead us out of our confusion, our fear and our anxiety. In today's complex world there are many other labyrinths in which we may lose ourselves: that of drugs, of eroticism, of alcohol, of food, and even of work. But for every maze we may face, God is prepared to lead us out and to receive us within his open arms.

Poppy: Ignorance

When we find ourselves lost, we need to stop to think and to take stock. To continue fleeing is to lose ourselves even more. If we stop to listen, we shall hear the "still, small voice." There is not a labyrinth in the world, in the cosmos, that can hide us from God. He is the Alpha and the Omega. He is the Beginning and the End, the Entrance and the Exit. He is the Way. When he whispers, "Come follow me," he is our golden string leading us to the peace that passes understanding.

and in the mist of tears

Weeping is a human act. It is healing in addition to being a call to action. In our hearts, we know we should not run from God and from his grace. We feel sorrow and at times we weep. We ask ourselves: Why have I turned away from God? Why haven't I been living a sacramental life? Why haven't I been praying? Why is it so hard to love my neighbor, myself, God?

Tears are a gift from our loving God as twentieth-century mystic, Maggie Ross, wrote:

> It cannot be emphasized enough that the gift of tears is a *gift*. Like any other gift, it can be accepted or rejected. While it cannot be forced or manipulated it can, like unceasing prayer of which it is a part, be

nurtured. It is an "ambient" grace. It is not the special possession of a spiritual elite but always available, waiting to find us receptive. It is an ineffable gift, and one of its distinguishing marks is that it always points us away from our selves even as it illuminates our selves.[1]

In despair and shame the speaker hides from Love in the "mist of tears," the very waters that are now preparing the soul for a rebirth and a return to the state of grace. As Ross said: "The gift of tears often comes at the moment of despair and the entering in of grace."[2]

I hid from Him, and under running laughter.

As if we could hide from God! There is no mist opaque enough to hide us from our Divine lover. The laughter mentioned in this verse is the nervous laughter of one who knows he is making a huge mistake in his life, following illusory pleasures that offer temporary escape from spiritual sickness. Partying, excessive drinking, illicit affairs are just other names for hiding and fleeing from God; the laughter is nothing but bravado, an immaturity that the soul must, in the end, face and resolve.

Sin's laughter is hollow and joyless. God alone offers us true joy and peace: "Peace I leave with you; my peace

I give to you. Not as the world gives do I give it to you" (Jn 14:27).

Up vistaed hopes I sped;

A vista is a view, usually one of an open space, a panoramic prospect, a great sight perhaps seen from a height. Here the speaker admits to blindly and swiftly following every pipe-dream springing from his opium-haunted mind. Many of us can identify with this verse. How many times have we been unrealistic in our expectations? How often have we deluded ourselves into being the kind of person God never meant us to be? How often has our ego become inflated with aspirations based upon vistas that our imagination has hatched and amplified beyond reasonable expectations? How often have we quickly dropped everything, our responsibilities to our family and friends and colleagues to follow these phantoms, all because of an unwillingness to face the truth about ourselves?

Often our "vistaed hopes" make us feel superior to others; but "vistaed hopes" are merely the aspirations of an inflated ego which sooner or later will deflate.

Seashell: Pilgrimage

And shot, precipitated,
Adown Titanic glooms of chasmèd fears,

When the ego is deflated, the soul plunges into "glooms": psychological depression. "Titanic" suggests the immensity of this fall into what is a state of being akin to despair.

Here, Thompson is at his spiritual and psychological nadir; he has hit bottom. We know that Thompson almost committed suicide because of his despair. We cannot say for sure that Thompson had entered a dark night of the soul, for he never lost his awareness of God's presence. But he refused to turn toward God; he fled blindly down the labyrinthine ways of his mind in a futile attempt to hide from God. Fortunately for all of us, the more we try to hide from God, the more God seeks us.

From those strong Feet that followed, followed after.

God's "strong Feet" unceasingly follow the soul. The metaphor of a "Hound" for God may seem strange, but the poet is keen on expressing the swift and untiring qualities of God's pursuit of souls. It reminds us of Christ's Good Shepherd parable: "Suppose one of you has a hundred sheep and loses one of them. Does he not leave the ninety-nine in the open country and go after the lost sheep until he finds it?" (Lk 15:4).

In a stroke of genius, Thompson masterfully employs synecdoche, a figure of speech that substitutes a part for the whole. Here, Thompson is referring only to those attributes of a hound that emphasize God's "doggedness," if you will, his unwillingness to give up the chase. We may give up on ourselves, but God never gives up on us. He follows until he finds his lost sheep.

> *But with unhurrying chase,*
> *And unperturbèd pace,*

For God there is no need for haste. It is we who are in a rush. But to go where? "Unperturbèd pace" again suggests how insistent God is in his love for us. We may say "no" to his summons, but then it is we who become perturbed, we who lose our peace of soul.

No one can outrun God. It is simpler and wiser to practice Jean-Pierre de Caussade's way of abandoning ourselves to "the joy of full surrender." Caussade said: "Aside from God's will, everything is hollow, empty, void: there is nothing but falsehood, vanity, nothingness, shallowness, the letter of the law, death."[3] In abandoning ourselves to the Divine, we find ourselves living according to Christ's words, "In losing yourself, you will find yourself" (cf. Mt 17:25).

Deliberate speed, majestic instancy,

Two more examples of oxymoron again remind us that God is totally Other. God's pursuit of souls is not one of whim but one deliberately entered upon. If his eye is on the sparrow, then it is certainly on us. So God's "deliberate speed" is an eternally patient pursuit, for God has loved us with an everlasting love from the beginning of time.

"Majestic" suggests all that is royal about God. He is King of Kings, and yet he does not view us as his subjects. No, we are his children. When Jesus prayed the Our Father, he employed the Aramaic diminutive for Father: Abba, which means Daddy. To others, a father may appear to be a King, but to his child, he is really the daddy who would kiss every curl of his child's head.

"Instancy" suggests urgency, derived from the Latin *instare*, meaning to press upon. Is there anything more urgent than salvation? What does it profit a person to gain the whole world and to lose oneself in the process? Augustine cried out, "Too late have I loved Thee." But that does not have to be the case with us. We can cease fleeing from our Lord, and turn toward him. Consider the parable of the Prodigal Son. The father runs toward his son who had been lost. There are no questions asked, no accusations, no "I told you so," no demand for an apology. Instead the father orders a celebration, the son is arrayed in the best of clothes and rings are placed upon his fingers. God's love is unconditional.

> *They beat—and a Voice beat*
> *More instant than the Feet—*

Again the poetic device of synecdoche. The feet of God still follow after us, and "feet" brings many images to mind: Christ washed the feet of his disciples, a ritual we still observe every Holy Thursday. What a beautiful gesture of love and humility our Lord used to illustrate his love for us! Then shortly after, Christ's own feet were nailed to the cross—again for love of us. Christ's feet are the feet of the Good Shepherd who would leave the ninety-nine to search for the one that is lost. The Shepherd's feet take him anywhere to retrieve what is of immense value to him: into brambles, up steep hills, to the edge of thorny crags, down into stony crevices.

The voice of God beats to our heartbeat. God's voice is also the voice of our conscience. How often we run away from this voice. Still, it follows us everywhere, like God's feet. The voice of God is one of Love. God's voice is attuned to our heartbeat, to the way we live our lives, to our moods, to our hopes, to our disappointments, to our joys.

"All things betray thee, who betrayest Me."

The speaker knows, likely from the very beginning of his flight from God, that anything he embraces that causes him to sin is a betrayal of his purpose in life.

When we sin, we betray not only what is best in ourselves, but we betray God. This choice is always ours. God will pursue us relentlessly, but in the end we must make a choice. Modern existentialism is based upon a philosophy of choice: it says our life is the result of our choices. Catholicism has taught this truth from the very beginning: we have free will. We can live by God's law of love or we can reject it. We can reject our Lord just as Judas rejected Christ with a kiss in the Garden of Gethsemane. Or, like Mary Magdalen, we can go and sin no more.

I pleaded, outlaw-wise,
By many a hearted casement, curtained red,
Trellised with intertwining charities;
(For, though I knew His love Who followèd,

Oak Branch: Knowledge

Yet was I sore adread
Lest, having Him, I must have naught beside);
But, if one little casement parted wide,
  The gust of His approach would clash it to.
  Fear wist not to evade, as Love wist to pursue.

Thompson candidly admits to sexual temptation. Having fled God's love and ignored God's law, he has become an outlaw, trying to outrun Love. So he turns to the usual substitute for real love: eroticism. What places are represented by a "hearted casement," windows "curtained in red"? He certainly is not referring to the stained-glass windows of cathedrals!

Every large city, including London, has what is often called the red light district. Such places are frequented by men searching for prostitutes. Surely Thompson knew the prostitutes of London's streets, and Thompson was a student of human nature. He saw Victorian gentlemen visit the poor sections of London where prostitutes resided. And he saw young women throwing their lives away, allowing themselves to be exploited. Eventually, he was appalled by the tragedy of these lives: both the pursuers and the pursued, and he lamented the squalor resulting from such living.

Thompson knew in his heart that his hunger for love could never be completely satisfied by any human being. He ran from his "tremendous Lover" because he was afraid that "having Him, I must have naught beside." However, there is a great mystery to God's love: once we have experienced it, we are never fully satisfied with anything less.

Augustine understood this profound truth. He reveled in the pleasures of the flesh before his conversion. Even when he was already attracted to God's love, he dared to pray that God allow him more time to sin: "Make me chaste, but not yet."[4] This sounds incredible, but if we carefully consider this ploy, we may recognize similar gambles in our own hearts: have we not begged God for certain favors, which, deep down, we know are not for our best? But God is the greatest "gambler" of all: from the beginning of time he gambles on us. Every time we agree to accept his will, he wins. Paradoxically, every time God wins, we also win!

We must accept the reality of the power of sin; it can take over a person; it can eventually destroy. However, the pleasures of sin are brief and fleeting. They do not offer true happiness; they simply offer respite from the real hunger that drives us: our hunger for the infinite, for God.

Across the margent of the world I fled,
And troubled the gold gateways of the stars,
Smiting for shelter on their clangèd bars;
Fretted to dulcet jars
And silvern chatter the pale ports o' the moon.
I said to Dawn: Be sudden—to Eve: Be soon;
With thy young skiey blossoms heap me over
From this tremendous Lover—
Float thy vague veil about me, lest He see!

Thompson's flight reaches beyond the "margent of the world." That is, he has fled beyond every border. In fact, he has departed the world and flown to the "gold gateways of the stars" and the "pale ports o' the moon." Such a great distance in order to outrun *The Hound of Heaven!* But there is no place in the cosmos where God is not present, for without God's love nothing in the cosmos could exist.

The medieval mystic Julian of Norwich understood God's enduring and ever-present love:

He showed me more, a little thing, the size of a hazelnut, on the palm of my hand, round like a ball. I looked at it thoughtfully and wondered, "What is this?" And the answer came, "It is all that is made." I marveled that it continued to exist and did not suddenly disintegrate; it was so small. And again

Arches and Clouds: Life Passages

my mind supplied the answer, "It exists both now and forever, because God loves it"; in short, everything owes its existence to the love of God.[5]

We have nowhere to go or to hide. There is no "vague veil" able to keep any of us from our "tremendous Lover." Each of us abides in God's loving, open palm. If, as the poet Anne Sexton said: "Touch is all," then we have nothing to fear: We are forever touched by God's love.

This stanza has impressed many critics because of its visionary scope. Some see in its imagery not so much a Victorian vision but a twentieth century cosmic vision. To Thompson, the sun, the moon, the stars, the planets and the galaxies are not faraway places. They exist within the soul, within the realm of the imagination. In the essay "Thompson's Space Rapture," biographer John Walsh wrote:

If imagery was the soul of Francis Thompson's poetry, then that soul had a soul of its own, for at the very center of his imagination there pulsed a radiant core that spread its kindling, iridescent influence over the greater part of his work. Even cursory analysis of his imagery shows that he was preoccupied to the point of rapture with the sublimity of transtellar space, with the heavenly bodies, and with all manner of celestial phenomena.[6]

Carl Sagan's novel *Contact* concerns mankind's first encounter with other beings. When the character Ellie Arroway is shot into space, she beholds the wonder of the universe in all of its glory. She repeats over and over, "It's so beautiful, it's so beautiful...." She also remarks that they should have sent into space not a scientist like herself but a poet, for only a poet could hope to capture in words such mystery and awesome beauty.

Yes, God's beauty is immense, but it is the poets who accept the challenge of making it real to all of us.

> *I sought no more that after which I strayed*
> > *In face of man or maid;*
> *But still within the little children's eyes*
> > *Seems something, something that replies,*
> *They at least are for me, surely for me!*
> *I turned me to them very wistfully;*

Sometimes we try to escape God by means of human relationships, that is, "In face of man or maid." We need our friends, our family, our spouses, those who support us. But human love will never serve as a substitute for God's love. We were made for Divine love.

Thompson must have quickly learned on the London streets, with its hustlers, pickpockets, prostitutes and thieves, that human sympathy is unreliable. But when sent by the Meynells to the priory at Storrington, Thompson enjoyed friendships in a new way with the rural children; they were a joy to him.

Perhaps in their innocence, Thompson saw a glimpse of his own former innocence. Surely children are a daily reminder of Christ's words, "Unless you are as one of these, you will not enter the kingdom of heaven" (cf. Mk 10:15). By all accounts there was something childlike about the poet Thompson; he was not a person layered in masks. Despite his problems, he was humble and kind; thus, children were drawn to him. In their eyes, he saw, "something, something that replies; *They* at least are for me, surely for me!" This is the lament of a man who saw the world as hostile, a place where he had experienced much rejection. In children, Thompson saw not rejection but acceptance. Fulton J. Sheen wrote:

> We all love little children, as Christ did. They are a revelation of God. God is in the artlessness of their ways, in the beauty of their eyes, and especially in the innocence of their hearts. God himself is, in a way, as a child, in his simplicity—there is nothing

complicated about him, and that is why it is so easy to serve him.[7]

We also know that Thompson became very close to the Meynell children. He wrote several poems dedicated to and about them, and was godfather to one of them. But something interfered with his friendship with God's little ones:

> *But just as their young eyes grew sudden fair*
> *With dawning answers there,*
> *Their angel plucked them from me by the hair.*

Thompson is perhaps not being completely honest here. It was not angels plucking the children away from him, but likely his own addiction to laudanum. Children are frightened by adults who appear drunk or disoriented; perhaps the poet's erratic manner when under the influence of laudanum frightened the children away.

Or, perhaps Thompson unconsciously drove children from his presence because he saw himself as a sinner, one who had fled from God's love. Perhaps he was unconsciously punishing himself, driving away from him the very people who brought so much joy into his life. There are other possible speculations, but one thing is certain: Thompson again was alone.

Now that he had rejected people in general, he sought to experience love by attention to natural beauty.

> *"Come then, ye other children, Nature's—share*
> *With me" (said I) "your delicate fellowship;*
> > *Let me greet you lip to lip,*
> > *Let me twine with you caresses,*
> > > *Wantoning*
> > *With our Lady-Mother's vagrant tresses,*
> > > *Banqueting*
> > *With her in her wind-walled palace,*
> > *Underneath her azured daïs,*
> > *Quaffing, as your taintless way is,*
> > > *From a chalice*
> *Lucent-weeping out of the dayspring."*
> > *So it was done:*
> *I in there delicate fellowship was one—*
> *Drew the bolt of Nature's secrecies.*

Thompson turns from people to embrace nature. He seeks in nature's beauty the companionship and nurturing that he hopes will render him happy. In fact, like many poets previous to Thompson, romantic poets like Wordsworth, Shelley and Keats, Thompson substitutes a worship of nature for religion, and this too will prove to be another dead end in his labyrinthine search for peace.

Cypresses: Death

Simone Weil, the twentieth-century Jewish mystic, said that God often uses beauty as a means to draw us back to him. Thompson becomes totally ensnared by nature's beauty; he knew the face of the sky as well as his own face.

I laughed in the morning's eyes.
I triumphed and I saddened with all weather,
Heaven and I wept together,
And its sweet tears were salt with mortal mine.
Against the red throb of its sunset-heart
I laid my own to beat,
And share commingling heat;

But fellowship with nature leaves him empty even though he has seemingly penetrated "nature's secrecies." He soon understands that nature cannot communicate with his soul because he cannot hear its words. "Their sound is but their stir, they speak by silences." As Augustine reminds us, only the ancient Beauty of God can satisfy our thirst.

The chalice of sweetness that nature offers is emptied all too soon, but Christ's chalice is forever overflowing. Nature, the poet concludes, is a "poor stepdame" who cannot "slake my drouth"—quench my thirst.

I stand amid the dust o' the mounded years—
My mangled youth lies dead beneath the heap,
My days have crackled and gone up in smoke,
Have puffed and burst as sun-starts on a stream.

Thompson is still not ready to return to his Lord, even though he sees the wreckage of his life heaped around him. So what is left the young man? His genius for poetry. But can poetry be a substitute for God?

Yea, faileth now even dream
The dreamer, and the lute the lutanist;
Even the linked fantasies, in whose blossomy
*   twist*
I swung the earth a trinket at my wrist,
Are yielding; cords of all too weak account
For earth with heavy griefs so overplussed.

The dreamer realizes that his dreams are delusions. The lutanist can no longer create music on his lute. The poet's words catch in his throat. The earth's beauty is like a "trinket at my wrist," an eye-catching bauble, but it no longer fulfills the poet's yearning. He has come to see the value of what Shakespeare calls the "eternal jewel"—the living soul. For the first time in the poem Thompson gives genuine thought to God,

> *Ah! is Thy love indeed*
> *A weed, albeit an amaranthine weed,*
> *Suffering no flowers except its own to mount?*
> *Ah! must—*
> *Designer infinite!—*
> *Ah! must Thou char the wood ere Thou canst*
> *limn with it?*

Thompson uses a negative image in addressing his Lord, but at least he has now turned his attention to God. Weeds are plants that choke up all other vegetation. We think of Hamlet's reference to Denmark as an "unweeded garden," but it was not so much Denmark that was unweeded as it was the mind and soul of Hamlet. The same is true of Thompson. His soul for the first time directly addresses God, "Ah! is Thy love indeed, A weed?" Here a weed is even a good thing, "an amaranthine weed" which will drive from the garden all the negative things that impair the growth of flowers. In other words, the poet's soul is preparing to flower.

God is the "Designer infinite!" God does what he must do for each of us. But there is a pattern, a mystical design. Before rebirth can take place, there needs to be a cleansing, a healing. The poet has suffered, he has not been happy. In fact, he has been miserable. He asks God, "Ah! must Thou char the wood ere Thou canst limn with it?" The answer to his question is "yes." The burning of wood is equivalent to the cleansing of the soul by suffering. But after the burning, the wood is transformed into the charcoal God can indeed use to draw his Divine image upon the soul.

When for the first time the poet faces the ravages of his sinful life, he is horrified by the years of his wasted youth,

> *My freshness spent its wavering shower i' the*
> *   dust;*
> *And now my heart is as a broken fount,*
> *Wherein tear-drippings stagnate, spilt down ever*
> *   From the dank thoughts that shiver*
> *Upon the sighful branches of my mind.*
> *   Such is; what is to be?*
> *The pulp so bitter, how shall taste the rind?*

The poet compares his heart to a "broken fount." His tears appear not to have been the waters of cleansing and rebirth; they are "stagnate." But such feelings of despair bring the stirrings of panic. If the pulp is so bitter, "how shall taste the rind?" In other words, if to follow God means eating bitter fruit, what must it be like to bite through what is required to get to that fruit: Is the rind even more bitter?

But here, the unspoken fear is the fear of the Cross. About this stanza Fulton J. Sheen wrote: "At the moment when he feels drawn to surrender to the Crucified, there comes before him, once again, a fear of submitting to the tortures of the Cross."[8]

> *Now of that long pursuit*
> *Comes on at hand the bruit;*
> *That Voice is round me like a bursting sea:*
> *"And is thy earth so marred,*
> *Shattered in shard on shard?*
> *Lo, all things fly thee, for thou fliest Me!*
> *Strange, piteous, futile thing!*
> *Wherefore should any set thee love apart?*
> *Seeing none but I make much of naught" (He*
>   *said),*
> *"And human love needs human meriting:*
> *How hast thou merited—*
> *Of all man's clotted clay the dingiest clot?"*

We are nearing the end of the chase. The "still, small voice" of the Lord has become a voice "round me like a bursting sea." The poet has no choice, no more evasion is possible, all escape routes have been tried. He is still.

Fountain with Turtles: Life

He listens. What does he hear? Simply a Voice telling him that even though he does not merit love, he *is* loved. Even though he is "naught"—nothing—God loves him nonetheless. Shakespeare's *King Lear* says to his daughter Cordelia, "Nothing will come of nothing," when she refuses to flatter his ego. But here, we are told that something can come of nothing. Although the speaker has been reduced to zero, God's eternal love transforms zero into infinity.

In this stanza, there is also an echo of Shakespeare's *Hamlet*. The Voice asks, "Of all man's clotted clay the dingiest clot?" Is man simply food for worms? In the play's famous graveyard scene, Hamlet holds in his hands the skull of "Poor Yorick," the court jester. Hamlet allows his imagination to ponder what happens to the human body after death. He even imagines that it can turn to clay to plug a beer barrel. Horatio warns Hamlet that it is unhealthy "to consider too curiously, to consider so."

But truly, we need to consider our lives, our purpose …and also our death. The poet himself has finally come to the conclusion that he is nothing without God. The world he has created for himself lies around him, "Shattered in shard on shard." The poet himself is a broken man.

But God is the "Designer infinite." He can restore what has been broken and transform it into beauty. God's love of us is not like human love. With God, love is unconditional. The poet now understands why all was taken from him, why he was reduced to zero. To return to the enfolding circle (zero) of God's embracing arms,

> *"All which I took from thee I did but take,*
> > *Not for thy harms,*
> *But just that thou might'st seek it in My arms."*

Now God invites home the one who has fled. God reaches out to the poet,

> *"Rise, clasp My hand, and come!"*

The great ode ends on a note of ambiguity. Does the speaker rise to clasp God's extended hand and loving embrace? We can only speculate. Such a response is based on choice, a choice we all have to make. God extends himself to each of us. He desperately longs to embrace us. The choice is before us. The choice is ours.

CHAPTER 6

The Hound of Heaven:
Transforming Power

My Own Discovery

A homeless man, standing every day outside the shop where I stop for my morning coffee, prompted my own return to Thompson's poetry years after my first reading. There he was without fail, in fair or in poor weather, with his hand outstretched for any change a stranger was willing to spare. I guessed he was in his mid-twenties, surely no more than thirty, but it is often difficult to guess the age of the homeless who often take upon themselves an ageless look defying calculation. His gaze was half focused on the real world. The other half, I surmised, fixed upon an inner vision to which only he was privy. Something about him moved me.

One cold day I looked more closely: he wore old, scruffy shoes with no socks; his pants were worn and ragged, and his bedraggled coat was more appropriate for spring rather than the frigid morning weather of a New England winter. He thanked me for the two quarters I dropped into his palm. His voice struck me as cultured, and I wondered about his background. He never spoke to me again, and shortly after that he disappeared. Every morning I looked for him, curious as to what had happened. If he were an addict, had he overdosed or had he been murdered on the perilous city streets? Had he been found somewhere dead from zero degree weather?

The faint memory of another man from another century haunted me: a man in broken shoes, no socks and wearing a coat without a shirt underneath. Later I recalled who my homeless man reminded me of: the mystic poet Francis Thompson.

Thompson's story swiftly returned to me, the story of the young genius who ended up homeless on the streets of London, a man of utter poverty reduced to selling matches, holding horses, and working as a bootblack for pennies. He slept along the fog bound Thames embankment or in a box at St. Martin-in-the-Fields church—a box eerily resembling a coffin—after he arrived on the London streets not long after his drug addiction had reduced his life to near non-existence. And yet, from this destitution came a man born to lift his poetic voice for all to hear.

At home, I rummaged through some boxes, found my dog-eared copy of *The Hound of Heaven*, and read it again for the first time since high school. I was in a spiritually arid place at that time in my life, yet when I read this verse my spirit stirred with optimism and joy. I experienced a glimmering awareness of God's love for me—for us. The radiance of my epiphany, initiated by *The Hound of Heaven,* grew within me and remained with me for days.

Others' Discovery

At the end of the great poem, *Rime of the Ancient Mariner,* the Mariner says:

> Farewell, farewell: but this I tell
> To thee, thou Wedding Guest!
> He prayeth well, who loveth well
> Both man and bird and beast.[1]

The Wedding Guest departs from the Mariner "A sadder and wiser man." Can poetry transform a man and render him wiser? Unlike those who argue that poetry changes nothing, I believe verse possesses the power to change lives for the better. As evidence, I offer the experiences of mystic Simone Weil (1909–1943); American playwright Eugene O'Neill (1888–1953); Dorothy Day (1897–1980), founder of the Catholic Worker Movement; and the famous painter, R. H. Ives Gammell (1893–1981).

Simone Weil

A famous twentieth century response to reading a religious poem is that of the Jewish mystical writer Simone Weil. When she visited the great monastery at Solemes to hear the monks' famed Gregorian chant, she met an Oxford undergraduate who introduced her to the seventeenth-century English metaphysical poet George Herbert. She chose Herbert's poem *Love Bade Me Welcome* and read it by "fixing all my attention on it and clinging with all my soul to the tenderness it enshrines." As she began reciting the poem to herself, her recitation became prayer. In this moment, when she and the poem merged in a marriage of attention, she experienced Christ. She wrote to a friend:

> I learned it by heart. Often, at the culminating point of a violent headache, I make myself say it over, concentrating all my attention upon it and clinging with all my soul to the tenderness it enshrines. I used to think I was merely reciting it as a beautiful poem, but without knowing it the recitation had the virtue of a prayer. It was during one of these recitations that Christ himself came down and took possession of me.[2]

In his study of Simone Weil, scholar George Abbot White says that one of the many moving photographs in Simone Petremont's biography of Weil is that of Herbert's *Love Bade Me Welcome*, copied by Weil. The handwriting is simple and beautiful: "it is neat, clear, without affectation. It is plain that in copying out the text she is concerned only with the poem, anxious that it be easily read, that nothing come between the reader and Christ's invitation to the sinner to the heavenly banquet."[3]

Through attentive reading and praying of poetry, many have received a great moment of grace in their lives. God can grant such graced moments to any of us through, in and by the beauty of poetry.

Eugene O'Neill

There are many striking similarities between Eugene O'Neill and Francis Thompson. Both were quite close to their devoutly Catholic mothers. O'Neill's mother had considered the vocation of religious life, as had Thompson's mother.

Both boys were active acolytes; both considered it a privilege to serve at the Eucharistic Celebration. Both boys had the touch of a poet in their souls (O'Neill wrote a play, *A Touch of the Poet*). Both were of delicate physical constitution; O'Neill suffered from tuberculosis as had Thompson. There seems to have been something self-destructive in both men, for each attempted suicide in their mid-twenties. O'Neill became an alcoholic, and Thompson was addicted to opium as well as alcohol.

O'Neill was born on October 16, 1888, coincidentally, the same year that Thompson first considered writing *The Hound of Heaven*. The young O'Neill, like Thompson, attended Catholic schools. In 1895 he enrolled at St. Aloysius, a boarding school taught by the Sisters of Charity of Riverdale, New York. He also attended De La Salle Institute in New York City, a school of the Christian Brothers.

In the summer of 1903 when O'Neill was 15, his mother Mary Ellen O'Neill threw herself into the Thames River outside her summer home in Connecticut. He discovered that his beloved mother had become addicted to morphine which she began taking when giving birth to her first child. That day changed O'Neill's life. Soon after his mother's suicide, Eugene O'Neill renounced his religious faith. He could not reconcile his anger with God, or his personal agony over the loss of his dear mother, with a belief in a loving God.

But that was not the end of religion in O'Neill's life.

Although he remained a lapsed Catholic for the rest of his life, his religious sensibility did not die, and like Thompson, O'Neill fled his God down the nights and down the days. Like Thompson whose life of degradation on the streets of London we can only imagine, O'Neill fled from his Lord down the alleys of New York's waterfronts, into the dark bars and brothels of the Bowery and into the nightmarish dream world of alcoholism. But always he carried within him Thompson's great poem.

One of the bars that O'Neill frequented in Greenwich Village had a back room called Hell Hole. When he had been drinking, O'Neill was well known for reciting Thompson's *The Hound of Heaven*—he knew all 182 verses by heart. One can imagine the darkness of the bar, the cold winter night outside and the dour, disconsolate O'Neill orating Thompson's majestic lines in a deep, introspective voice. It is recorded that the playwright intoned the verse with emotion. Why had he memorized the lines to begin with? We only take within ourselves verses that speak to us, verses we identify with, that offer us consolation.

Doris Alexander offers an insightful interpretation of

what *The Hound of Heaven* meant to the young Eugene O'Neill:

> In Thompson's flight from love and God, in his search for meaning, in his urgent images of running and hiding, always pursued by what he fled until he came full circle back to faith, O'Neill saw his own flight from his parents' love and from his boyhood religious faith; he saw all his years of wandering and intellectual searching, his despair…his divorce, his suicide attempt, and his return to his family just before the tuberculosis got him.[4]

One of his great plays *Days without End* is based upon O'Neill's favorite poem *The Hound of Heaven*. It is the story of John Loving, a divided soul who was near despair until one day his uncle, a priest named Father Baird, shows up unannounced. His uncle somehow felt that Loving's soul was in danger.

Father Baird: Do you know Francis Thompson's poem, *The Hound of Heaven?*

Loving: I did once. Why?

Father Baird (quotes in a low voice but with deep feeling):

"Ah, fondest, blindest, weakest,
I am He Whom thou seekest!
Thou dravest love from thee, who dravest Me."

Loving (in what is close to a snarl of scorn): Love!

Father Baird: Why do you run and hide from him, as from an enemy? Take care. There comes a time in every man's life when he must have his God for friend, or he has no friend at all, not even himself. Who knows? Perhaps you are on the threshold of that time now.[5]

John Loving was on that threshold. On stage he is presented as two people: "John" and "Loving"—symbolic of a divided self. He is the man running from Love. Only when he surrenders to Christ's love at the foot of the cross in a church, does the character find wholeness: only in losing himself does he again become John Loving. The false self dies so that the true self emerges. John Loving's last words are "Life laughs with God's love again! Life laughs with love!"

Most of O'Neill's plays are autobiographical. He understood that he was in flight from God and that this flight was the root of his unhappiness.

Dorothy Day

Along his journey, O'Neill was used by God to touch the soul of another person, one also lost in the labyrinthine ways of her own mind: Dorothy Day. Day, along with Peter Maurin, founded the Catholic Worker movement in America in 1932; she, along with Merton, is one of this centuries most famous converts to Catholicism. She was born on Pineapple Street in Brooklyn Heights on November 8, 1897. Like O'Neill, Day frequented Greenwich Village's Hell Hole, where the artists, writers and theater players congregated. Here, one night, she found her first link with Catholicism when O'Neill began to recite Thompson's poem, *The Hound of Heaven*, within earshot of Day. According to Dorothy Day herself, she was never the same woman:

> Late one night in the "Hell Hole" as Wallace's back room was called, O'Neill, quite drunk, recited Francis Thompson's poem *The Hound of Heaven*. Gene could recite all of it. He used to sit there, looking dour and black, his head sunk on his chest, sighing, "And now my heart is a broken fount wherein tear-drippings stagnate." It was one of those poems that awaken the soul, recalls to it the fact that God

is its destiny. The idea of this pursuit fascinated me, the inevitableness of it, the recurrence of it, made me feel that inevitably I would have to pause in the mad rush of living to remember my first beginning and last end. [6]

When she heard O'Neill's recitation, Day said no one "knew how profoundly moved I was. I did my best to hide it, but I was again 'tormented by God.'"[7]

In *Told in Context*, Dorothy Day remembered Eugene O'Neill, the man she had known 40 years before:

To me, he portrayed more than any other, what life without God is like. "Without redemption, how great a tragedy ever to be born," Newman wrote.

Gene seemed always to be setting his will against God. Since he brought to me such a consciousness of God, since he recited to me *The Hound of Heaven*, I owe him my prayers.[8]

R. H. Ives Gammell

The American artist R. H. Ives Gammell was born in 1893 to a wealthy family of bankers in Rhode Island. From the age of ten he desired to be a painter, but his family disapproved of his artistic vocation. Eventually, he convinced them to allow him to enroll at the Boston Museum School of Fine Arts and, in 1913, he left America to spend a year in Paris studying the Old Masters.

Gammell's most productive years were the 1930s when he was commissioned to do several portraits and murals. Painting murals sparked his lifelong interest in allegorical pictures which culminated in his most famous work *The Hound of Heaven: A Pictorial Sequence*. The sequence constitutes Gammell's *magnum opus*: twenty-one panels measuring 6' 7" x 2' 7" which portray the narrative of a soul's flight from and return to God.

Gammell first read Thompson's ode when he was sixteen. Even at such a young age he identified with the poem and for a lifetime was haunted by the richness of its imagery and message. Although Gammell was raised an Episcopalian, he renounced formal religion as a young man; yet he never lost his essentially religious sensibility.

In 1939 Gammell suffered a nervous breakdown which coincided with the outbreak of World War II. This crisis brought him back to Thompson's ode, which he had always hoped to represent pictorially. He writes of this tremendous creative endeavor:

> Over a long period of years Francis Thompson's poem evoked in my mind pictorial ideas for which I remained unable to find imagery susceptible of con-

veying my meaning. The reconstituted Medieval-ism which a literal reading suggested was particu-larly foreign to my purpose.

Eventually I decided that it would involve only a slight change in terminology to consider *The Hound of Heaven* as a history of the experience com-monly called emotional breakdown rather than as the story of a specifically religious conversion. The change did not, it seemed to me, traduce the poet's intention; it suggested, however, a construction ca-pable of conveying the universality of his subject to many persons who might otherwise think its appli-cation limited to individuals professing a particular creed.

At any rate this interpretation immediately brought within range a quantity of pictorial ideas which had haunted my thought for many years but which I had never found a connecting link capable of giving them artistic unity.[9]

Gammell recognized himself in Thompson's poem, and it is the universal nature of the poem that continues speaking to people of every century. Both the painter Gammell and the poet Thompson speak to our time of confusion, fear and alienation because they both remind us of God's love for each of us, a love that never ceases to pursue us.

Gammell saw in Thompson's poem the terror-filled flight into darkness, and he saw all the substitutes we turn to in this flight from God. He saw our fear of death and our self-loathing. But he also saw in Thompson's moving verse God's unconditional love for his children.

Gammell's pictorial interpretation of *The Hound of Heaven* enriches our understanding of this profound poem because it takes the poem's highly symbolic nature and adds to it a new layer of interpretation: the findings of modern psychology. Gammell admitted that he owed his own psychic survival to Thompson's poem; his pictorial sequence is his expression of gratitude.

Eugene O'Neill, Dorothy Day, R. H. Ives Gammell. Is it not miraculous that these three lives should be so intertwined with Francis Thompson's life? In Thornton Wilder's philosophical novel, *The Bridge of San Luis Rey,* Brother Juniper tracked down the lives and all the connections among the seven people who fell from a bridge to their deaths, in an attempt to explain the incomprehensible events of life. I cannot play the role of Brother Juniper here, but I am sure that the poem *The Hound of*

Heaven is a bridge of love, leading many into the arms of God. Thompson himself came to the same conclusion as Thornton Wilder: "There is a land of the living, and the land of the dead, and the bridge is love, the only survival, the only meaning."[10]

Perhaps that is why God inspired Thompson to write the poem; perhaps that is why it haunted O'Neill; why Dorothy Day was in that bar on that particular day to hear it; why Gammell's emotional turmoil led him to such creativity. Who knows how many more will be forever changed by this magnificent poem of God's unconditional love?

CHAPTER 7

Poetry: A Way
of Life-Long Learning

Students of Poetry

Teaching high school literature has given me a certain awe for the way poetry, and in particular *The Hound of Heaven*, can reach both young and old.

I was almost finished with the unit on Victorian poetry. My students and I had closely studied Tennyson's *Ulysses*, Browning's *My Last Duchess*, Arnold's *Dover Beach*, Hopkins's *Pied Beauty*, and Hardy's *The Darkling Thrush*. In my first lecture I mentioned that all these poets had suffered some kind of religious crisis that led them either to faith or to agnosticism. I was curious to see their possible responses to an intensely mystical poem, so I gave out copies of Thompson's *The Hound of Heaven*. Reading the poem aloud didn't prevent my noticing the utter quiet and unusual stillness of my students. After I finished, I gave them Thompson's biography, and asked my students to read the poem again on their own, to write an analysis of the first stanza, and to offer an opinion of the poem in general.

Their opinions ranged from appreciation to indifference to outright rejection. The majority of my students found the poem a challenge to read, and many of them said they liked it. One young Irish student complained about "some extremely confusing language," but then confided that she well understood the ups and downs of a drug-haunted life, the highs of "vistaed hopes" and the subsequent crashings of "Titanic glooms." An Hispanic young man said, "This poem is incredibly powerful because it's so personal yet so broad…. I like this poem. It's the first poem I've read that really makes sense." An Asian girl wrote, "Even though I don't believe in God, it is touching to see how those who do believe in God know that he will always be following them and will be there whenever they need someone to turn to." A quiet young man responded, "We all have had our doubts and fears, but we know that he is with us all the time and will help us through our problems."

Another student observed, "This poem talks about

the hardships of homelessness and drug addiction, things that Thompson had experienced. Thompson sees that God and love are the solution to his problems. I like the poem because I believe what Thompson says is true." Other essays addressed belief and non-belief, running away from problems, the "maze-way" of drug usage, forgiveness and the power of love.

The teenagers were also intrigued by the poet's conflict with his father, his indecision about a profession, his succumbing to the lure of temptation. Perhaps they could relate to these from personal experience. Referring to the poem's extraordinary metaphor, one student said that her father was like "a hound" but that she understood his hounding as the result of his love for her; thus, she could relate to a God who also hounds. Most of my students concluded that the insight gained was worth facing the obscurity and esoteric choice of words and the far-fetched splendor of Thompson's imagery.

Needless to say my students' essays were gratifying. They proved to me that even today Thompson's poetry retains its power to communicate, because it was written not only from imagination and belief, but also from lived experience. When Thompson wrote that he fled God "down the nights and down the days," he meant it. And when he said: "All things betray thee, who betrayest Me," he knew it because he lived it.

And if his words can speak across a hundred years to our rather sophisticated high school students, then surely Thompson can speak to us as well. The literary critic David Perkins writes that in Thompson's verse, "We hear the nineteenth-century poet voicing his terror, frustration, regret, and longing, and struggling toward acceptance and hope."[1] These are the concerns of each of us as well.

When we reach adulthood, we don't cease being students. We are always learning; in fact, we need to retain the curious and searching mind of the student if we are to grow spiritually. Before poetry, we are to be like humble students.

Poetry as "Sacred Ground"

Spiritual transformations sometimes have happened because of contact with "sacred ground." I think of Thomas Merton who visited the splendid churches of Rome and for the first time wanted to know Christ. I think of Wallace Stevens sneaking into St. Patrick's Cathedral on his trips to New York just to sit in its holy ambiance. While gathering wood for a fire, World War I poet and artist David Jones saw a light gleaming from a barn; peeking through boards, he observed the Eucharist being celebrated with soldiers reverently on their knees— a sight that changed his life forever. Another great World War I poet, Siegfried Sassoon, converted to Catholicism late in life. In a poetic account of his conversion, *Lenten Illuminations*, he wrote: "What were you up to—going into churches all those years, / Of faith unfaithful?"[2] A more recent poet, Denise Levertov, also confesses to surreptitious visitations to churches, "At first, belief was a joy I kept secret, stealing into sacred places."[3]

We know that the "sacred ground" is not only contained within the stone and wood architecture of churches; we may also find it in spiritual poetry. When we decide to pray a poem, we enter sacred ground where the holy can happen.

There is much religious poetry available to us today. To benefit the most from a prayerful experience of poetry, careful attention to our frame of mind is most important. When we enter into praying a poem, we bring with us what twentieth-century philosopher J. Krishnamurti calls our "religious mind: the investigation, with all one's attention, with the summation of all one's energy, to find that which is sacred, to come upon that which is holy."[4] When we pray poetry we create our own oratory of the heart and mind where both the poet and the reader engage in dialogue.

When entering the "sacred ground" of poetry be prepared for anything to happen. One thing is bound to occur. We become attentive to the NOW moment. Whether or not we are allowed a glimpse of the *mysterium tremendum*—the tremendous mystery—is something to be hoped for but not demanded. Such an experience is truly a gift of God's grace.

CHAPTER 8

Ten Steps to Reading
Poetry in a Holy Way

I offer the following ten steps in the sincere hope that epiphany—that radical, life-changing moment—may be yours as you embark upon your prayerful, poetic journey.

1. Choose a poem to pray. Do not be concerned whether it is a religious poem or a secular one. Every great poem's source is the soul; therefore, it is a gift of grace and can speak to your own soul.

2. Choose a quiet place. In silence and solitude, create your own oratory of heart and mind where you can be alone with the poem. Picture yourself as a contemplative before a holy reading.

3. If possible, read the poem aloud. Poetry, like God's Word, is meant to be heard. Often, a poem reveals its deeper meaning when spoken.

4. Focus your attention completely on the poem, putting aside distractions. When you give yourself to a poem, you enter into an act of meditation which has the potential of becoming a moment of grace, if not a moment of transformation.

5. If you feel inspired to do so, look up the definitions of the words you don't understand, but try not to be obsessive about complete comprehension. Poetry has the power to communicate even when one doesn't understand every word.

6. Take note of capitalization and punctuation which may serve as important clues to the deeper meaning of the poem.

7. If helpful, take note of the poetic devices used, such as metaphor, simile, alliteration, onomatopoeia, assonance, consonance, hyperbole, etc. Attention to poetic figures of speech may enhance your appreciation of the poem's layered meaning.

8. After sitting quietly with the verses, reread your chosen poem. A second reading may open your heart to something that your attention previously missed and thus, you may understand the poem more deeply.

9. Do not become discouraged if you feel you haven't plumbed the meaning of the poem. You have not wasted your time; as Simone Weil once said: "Never in any case whatever is a genuine effort of attention wasted. It always has its effect on the spiritual plane and in consequence, on the lower one of the intelligence, for all spiritual light enlightens the mind."[1]

10. When a poem speaks to you, you should memorize it so that its spiritual power is always available to you; thus, as a mantra or a prayer, it can center you, calm you, or inspire you whenever you need it most.

Suggested Poems for Prayer

Auden, W. H.
  Prime

Berryman, John
  Eleven Addresses to the Lord

Borges, Jorge Luis
  Luke XXIII

Brooke, Rupert
  Mary and Gabriel

Daly, Padraig J.
  Elegy at Mornington

Eliot, T. S.
  Little Gidding

Farren, Robert
  Stable Straw

Herbert, George
Love Bade Me Welcome

Hopkins, G. M.
God's Grandeur
The Habit of Perfection
Pied Beauty

Hudgins, Andrew
Ecce Homo
Gospel

Kiely, Jerome
For a Young Cistercian Monk

Kinsella, Thomas
The Monk

Levertov, Denise
Daily Bread
On a Theme from Julian's Chapter XX

Logan, John
Monologue for the Good Friday Christ

Mariani, Paul
Then Sings My Soul

Sassoon, Siegfried
The Tasking
Unfoldment

Sexton, Anne
Small Wire

Stevens, Wallace
Final Soliloquy of the Interior Paramour

Thomas, R. S.
The Presence
Suddenly

Wilbur, Richard
A Wedding Toast

Wylie, Elinor
Peter and John

Interpretive Artwork

by Anthony Lobosco

Based on the spiritual themes found in *The Hound of Heaven*, this painting artistically represents the journey of every Christian. The Christian pilgrim, sitting near a seashell, (symbol of pilgrimage), listens to the voice of wisdom, portrayed as a figure in red. He reads the book of life, in which his story is incomplete. The unfinished column behind the pilgrim shows the story of salvation history, beginning with Adam and Eve. As pilgrims, we all must embrace an individual journey toward wholeness, completing the column with our lives.

The incompleteness of life-in-process is also seen in the arches over the river: half-circles. Like the pilgrim standing in meditation on the bridge, we are often caught between water and sky, between things of heaven and things of earth. The circle of life is completed in the joining of the two, as the water-reflection of the arches meet the stone arches to form a whole.

Water nurtures life, like Divine grace which animates spiritual life. Springing up in a fountain, it cleanses and refreshes the journeying spirit. The water lilies recall the beauty of the soul resting upon the water of grace, and the fountain turtles symbolize the integration of the outer and inner self, the unity of nature and grace.

Along the spiritual way, the pilgrim will encounter spiritual danger, represented by red poppies. Despite the unknown, the pilgrim continues to ascend the stairs of life, which at times weave in and out in a labyrinthine maze.

The cypress and oak trees recall themes of light and darkness. The oak branch represents knowledge which brings strength; the cypress represents death: the death to selfishness necessary for life in God.

The angels holding the instruments of Christ's passion remind us that, while we cannot escape the reality of suffering, we live these dark moments mysteriously participating in Christ's paschal mystery.

The end of every journey is God, here portrayed in radiant, sun-drenched splendor, truly the Alpha and the Omega, the Light of the World.

Notes

Introduction

1. Thomas Merton, *No Man Is an Island* (New York: Harcourt, Brace, Jovanovich, 1953), p. 34.

Chapter 1
Why Poetry?

1. Mary Oliver, *New and Selected Poems* (Boston: Beacon Press, 1992), p. 10.

2. Kathleen Raine, *The Inner Journey of the Poet* (New York: George Braziller, 1982), p. 24.

3. Simone Weil, *The Simone Weil Reader*, ed., George A. Panichas (New York: David McKay Co., 1977), p. 45.

4. Thomas Merton, *Run to the Mountain* (San Francisco: HarperSanFrancisco, 1995), p. 53.

5. John Dewey, *Art As Experience* (New York: 1980), p. 195.

6. Denise Levertov, *New and Selected Essays* (New York: A New Directions Book, 1992), p. 150.

7. Howard Nemerov, *Poets on Poetry* (New York: Basic Books, Inc., 1966), p. 210.

8. Kathleen Raine, *The Inner Journey of the Poet* (New York: George Braziller, 1982), p. 32.

9. Carl Jung, *Psychological Reflections: A New Anthology,* ed. Jolande Jacobi and R. F. C. Hull (New York: Bollingen Foundation 1953), p. 202.

10. Raissa Maritain, *Raissa's Journal* (New York: Magi Books, 1974), p. 374.

11. Mary Oliver, *White Pine: Poems and Prose Poems* (New York: Harcourt Brace, 1994), p. 8.

12. Robert Sardello, *Facing the World with a Soul,* (New York: HarperCollins, 1992), p. 56.

Chapter 2
The Hound of Heaven: A Spiritual Autobiography

1. John Walsh, *The Letters of Francis Thompson* (New York: Hawthorne Books Inc., 1969), p.192.

2. John Walsh, *Strange Harp, Strange Symphony: The Life of Francis Thompson* (New York: Hawthorn Books, Inc., 1967), pp. 74–75.

3. Ibid., p. 73.

4. Rev. Terence L Connolly, ed., *Poems of Francis Thompson, Ode to the Setting Sun* (New York: The Century Co., 1932), p. 82.

5. Ibid., p. 5.

6. John Walsh, *Strange Harp, Strange Symphony: The Life of Francis Thompson* (New York: Hawthorn Books, Inc., 1967), p. 76.

Chapter 3
The Hound of Heaven: Mystical Literature

1. John Thompson, *Francis Thompson: Poet and Mystic* (London: Simpkins, Marshall, Hamilton, Kent and Co., Ltd., 1912), pp. 49–50.

2. Ibid.

3. Ibid.

4. Ibid.

5. James Dickey, *Babel to Byzantium* (New York: Farrar, Straus and Giroux, 1968), p. 241.

6. Fulton J. Sheen, *Lift Up Your Heart* (New York: Image Books, 1955), p. 252.

7. R. S. Pine-Coffin, ed., *St. Augustine's* Confessions (London: Penguin Classics, 1961), Book X.

8. Percy Herbert Osmond, *The Mystical Poets of the English Church* (New York: Macmillan, 1919), p. 340.

9. Louis Untermeyer, *Lives of the Poets* (New York: Simon and Schuster, 1959), p. 603.

Chapter 5
The Hound of Heaven: A Meditation

1. Maggie Ross, *The Fountain and the Furnace: The Way of Tears and Fire* (New Jersey: Paulist Press, 1987), pp. 147–149.

2. Ibid.

3. Pierre De Caussade, *The Joy of Full Surrender* trans. Hal L. Helms (Orleans: Paraclete Press, 1986), p. 19.

4. R. S. Pine-Coffin, ed., *St. Augustine's* Confessions (London: Penguin Classics, 1961), Book X.

5. Dame Julian of Norwich, *Revelations of Divine Love* (London: Penguin, n.d.), p. 64.

6. John Walsh, *Strange Harp, Strange Symphony: The Life of Francis Thompson* (New York: Hawthorn Books Inc., 1967), p. 227.

7. Fulton J. Sheen, *Text and Notes:* The Hound of Heaven (n.p., n.d.), p. 46.

8. Ibid., p. 60.

Chapter 6
The Hound of Heaven: Transforming Power

1. Samuel Taylor Coleridge, *Rime of the Ancient Mariner* in *Immortal Poems of the English Language*, ed. Oscar Williams (New York: Simon and Schuster Inc., 1952), p. 269.

2. Richard Rees, *A Sketch for a Portrait* (Southern Illinois University Press, 1966), pp. 58–59.

3. George Abbot White, *Interpretations of a Life* (Boston: The University of Massachusetts Press, 1981), pp. 38–39.

4. Doris Alexander, *Eugene O'Neill's Creative Struggle: The Decisive Decade 1924–1933* (University Park, Pennsylvania State University Press, 1992), p. 191.

5. Eugene O'Neill, *Days without End* (New York: Randon House, 1934).

6. William D. Miller, *All Is Grace: The Spirituality of Dorothy Day* (Garden City, N. Y., 1987), pp. 13–14.

7. Ibid.

8. William A. Miller, *Dorothy Day: A Biography;* Dorothy Day, Told in Context, (San Fransico: Harper and Row, 1982), p. 6.

9. *The Hound of Heaven: A Pictorial Sequence,* introduction and commentaries by Brigid M. Boardman (Boston: Sigo Press, 1994), p. 2.

10. Thornton Wilder, *The Bridge of San Louis Rey* (New York: Albert and Charles Boni, 1927), p. 235.

Chapter 7
Poetry: A Way of Life-Long Learning

1. David Perkins, *A History of Modern Poetry* (Cambridge: Harvard University Press, 1976), p. 21.

2. Siegfried Sassoon, *Selected Poems* (London: Faber and Faber, 1968), p. 82.

3. Denise Levertov, *The Stream and the Sapphire* (New York: New Directions, 1997), p. 15.

4. J. Krishnamurti, *The Wholeness of Life* (San Francisco: Harper and Row, 1979), p. 145.

Chapter 8
Ten Steps to Reading Poetry in a Holy Way

1. Simone Weil, George A. Panichas, ed., *The Simone Weil Reader* (New York: David McKay Co., 1977), p. 45.

Selected Bibliography

De la Gorce, *Francis Thompson*. London: Burns Oates and Washbourne LTD., 1933.

Megroz, R. L. *Francis Thompson: The Poet of Earth in Heaven.* London: Faber and Gwyer, 1927.

Sheen, Fulton J. *Lift Up Your Heart.* New York: Image Books, 1955, p. 252.

Thomson, John. *Francis Thompson: Poet and Mystic.* London: Simpkins Marshall, Hamilton Kent and Co., LTD., 1912.

Wright, T. H. *Francis Thompson and His Poetry.* London: George G. Harrap and Co., LTD., 1927.

BOOKS & MEDIA

The Daughters of St. Paul operate book and media centers at the following addresses. Visit, call or write the one nearest you today, or find us on the World Wide Web, www.pauline.org

CALIFORNIA
3908 Sepulveda Blvd., Culver City, CA
  90230; 310-397-8676
5945 Balboa Ave., San Diego, CA
  92111; 858-565-9181
46 Geary Street, San Francisco, CA
  94108; 415-781-5180

FLORIDA
145 S.W. 107th Ave., Miami, FL
  33174; 305-559-6715

HAWAII
1143 Bishop Street, Honolulu, HI
  96813; 808-521-2731
Neighbor Islands call: 800-259-8463

ILLINOIS
172 N. Michigan Ave., Chicago, IL
  60601; 312-346-4228

LOUISIANA
4403 Veterans Blvd., Metairie, LA
  70006; 504-887-7631

MASSACHUSETTS
Rte. 1, 885 Providence Hwy.,
  Dedham, MA 02026;
  781-326-5385

MISSOURI
9804 Watson Rd., St. Louis, MO
  63126; 314-965-3512

NEW JERSEY
561 U.S. Route 1, Wick Plaza,
  Edison, NJ 08817;
  732-572-1200

NEW YORK
150 East 52nd Street, New York, NY
  10022; 212-754-1110
78 Fort Place, Staten Island, NY
  10301; 718-447-5071

OHIO
2105 Ontario Street (at Prospect
  Ave.), Cleveland, OH 44115;
  216-621-9427

PENNSYLVANIA
9171-A Roosevelt Blvd., Philadelphia,
  PA 19114; 215-676-9494

SOUTH CAROLINA
243 King Street, Charleston, SC
  29401; 843-577-0175

TENNESSEE
4811 Poplar Ave., Memphis, TN
  38117 901-761-2987

TEXAS
114 Main Plaza, San Antonio, TX
  78205; 210-224-8101

VIRGINIA
1025 King Street, Alexandria, VA
  22314; 703-549-3806

CANADA
3022 Dufferin Street, Toronto, Ontario,
  Canada M6B 3T5;
  416-781-9131
1155 Yonge Street, Toronto, Ontario,
  Canada M4T 1W2;
  416-934-3440

¡También somos su fuente para libros, videos y música en español!